EDITORIAL RESEARCH REPORTS ON THE

AMERICAN WORK ETHIC

4049 7c

Published by Congressional Quarterly, Inc.
1735 K Street, N.W.
Washington, D.C. 20006

About the Cover

Jack Barrett, the cover's graphic designer, por-trays the robot-like quality of the assembly line by rendering clothespins into the image of faceless work-men. The design, photographed by Barrett and Frazier Hale, was under the overall supervision of George Sweers and Howard E. Chapman.

Published in March 1973

Library of Congress Catalogue Card Number 72-94080
International Standard Book No. 0-87187-042-8

Editorial Research Reports
Editor Emeritus, Richard M. Boeckel
Editor, William B. Dickinson, Jr.
Managing Editor, Hoyt Gimlin
Production Supervisor, Richard C. Young

CONTENTS

FOREWORD

This book explores the widening problem of making people want to work. It seems that the old American work ethic may be failing, or at least slipping, and there is no consensus whether this is for better or worse. The Puritans brought with them the Calvinist conviction that hard-earned success was a sign of God's grace. The religious aspect has dimmed over the years but there is no doubt that the idea was firmly planted in the American consciousness.

Now contrast that idea with present-day reality. As portrayed in a host of official studies, press findings and industry reports, the increasingly familiar "blue-collar blues" of bored, alienated assembly-line workers have spread to a white-collar world of dull, unchallenging jobs. There is fear that worker discontent is so pervasive it may undermine the nation's social and economic structure.

These gloomy accounts and warnings lend themselves to various explanations. One is that affluence, hedonism and radicalism have turned young people away from the capitalist system and its lure of material success. Another is that workers become bored more easily as they become better educated. Still another view is that workers, especially the young, have learned to expect more personal satisfaction from their careers. Industry is responding, here and there, to demands for shorter work weeks, better working conditions, and even a rearrangement of production lines to make the work less stultifying. As an example of this trend, new union contracts to be negotiated in Detroit this summer are expected to emphasize job quality even more than pay increases.

And yet the American worker is able to confound the experts who measure, gauge, index and analyze his discontent. It is noted that he cast his support in 1972 for a President who extolled the work ethic. As expressed by President Nixon in the election campaign, "We are faced with a choice between the work ethic...and the new welfare ethic..." Thus the work ethic has assumed a political coloration. And that coloration is not likely to fade in the year 1973 as the administration sets out to limit or dismantle many of the social and welfare programs enacted over the past four decades.

Hoyt Gimlin
Managing Editor

March 1973
Washington, D.C.

PRODUCTIVITY AND THE NEW WORK ETHIC

by

Ralph C. Deans

1 9 7 2
Apr. 19

PRODUCTIVITY AND THE NEW WORK ETHIC

E CONOMISTS HAVE BEGUN to identify poor productivity growth as the root cause of many other economic ills. They contend that the efficiency of American workers, if not actually declining, is at least not growing as fast as it was in the past or as fast as that of workers in other countries. Although productivity began lagging in the mid-Sixties, wages continued to go up. These are viewed as the major factors in America's persistant inflation and the failure of American goods to compete in foreign and domestic markets.

Furthermore, some economists believe that changes in the economy and in public attitudes toward jobs, the environment and technology may mean that future large-scale increases in productivity will be difficult, if not impossible, to achieve. Of particular concern is that a new work ethic is taking hold, especially among young workers. This implies the rejection of such an ingrained national ideal as hard work being its own reward. There is fear that the United States might have to resign itself permanently to a lower standard of living, with all the social, political and economic implications it would entail.

The "productivity crisis" theory is highly speculative and many, perhaps most, economists believe the way can be found to maintain the traditional growth of American efficiency. If workers are now disenchanted with their jobs and no longer idealize hard work, it is argued, then job-enrichment programs, technological advances and shorter workweeks might lessen the impact of that trend. Systems analysis and sophisticated managerial techniques might be brought to bear on such service industries as retailing, education and government to make them more efficient. It is also argued that the high productivity increases in other countries will eventually tail off and that American goods will consequently become competitive again.

Both sides in this debate rely on the same statistics. Output per man-hour—the most commonly used gauge of productivity—increased by an average of more than 3 per cent a year from the end of World War II to 1965. But the average annual increase fell to 2.1 per cent during the 1965-70 period. That decline is the basis for much of the concern now being expressed, even though productivity rebounded in 1971 *(see table, p. 13)* and is widely forecast to improve again this year. Those who continue to see a "productivity crisis" recall that productivity usually increases during a business recovery. They suggest that the current increases only mask a long-term trend in the opposite direction.

Nixon's Stress on Need to Increase Productivity

Productivity has become a major object of concern in the Nixon administration. On June 17, 1970, the President said he intended to create the National Commission on Productivity to "give first priority to the problems we face now...[to] achieve a balance between costs and productivity that will lead to more stable prices." [1] In his economic report to Congress on Jan. 27, 1972, the President said rising productivity was "the fundamental task of the American economy." And at a White House businessmen's conference the following month, he asked: "Are you going to crawl into a shell and demand protection, or are you going to roll up your sleeves and increase productivity?" It has been estimated that in the federal budget requests submitted to Congress for fiscal 1973, some $17.8 billion would be devoted to increased productivity through technological advances and expanded programs for the Productivity Commission. [2]

The administration is relying heavily on the Productivity Commission to find ways to improve productivity. In a policy statement it issued Sept. 7, 1971, the commission said that "the first and basic prerequisite" for productivity improvement was "an expanding economy, with maximum employment and maximum utilization of plants and machines." The commission identified six "targets of opportunity" which the nation had to aim at in order to raise productivity performance. They were:

Productivity bargaining in new labor contracts *(see page 16)*.

Strengthening of manpower adjustment programs to avoid the displacement of workers by automation.

Stimulation of research and development.

---

[1] The first commission members were named July 10, 1970. There are at present eight each from business, labor, the public at large, and the government. Peter G. Peterson, the new Secretary of Commerce, succeeded George P. Shultz, director of the Office of Management and Budget, as chairman, Feb. 29, 1972.

[2] Estimate of *U.S. News & World Report*, Feb. 7, 1972, p. 67.

INDEX 1950 - 100
(RATIO SCALE)

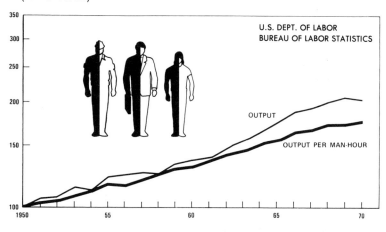

Improvement of productivity in government.

Policies to ensure an adequate supply of capital for economic growth.

Identification of industries with lagging productivity growth.

Productivity is also a central element in the administration's economic stabilization program [3] and the Phase II controls placed on wages and prices by the Cost of Living Council, the Pay Board and the Price Commission. The primary duty of these agencies is to hold down inflation, but they are relying largely on productivity increases to do it. Companies applying to the Price Commission to raise prices must include productivity data with their requests. C. Jackson Grayson Jr., chairman of the commission, told businessmen in January 1972 that "the length of time you're going to have controls is almost directly proportionate to the length of time it takes to get American productivity on the rise again." [4]

Grayson's admonition came despite a hefty increase in output per man-hour during the last quarter of 1971. His point may have been that the rate of increase—4.9 per cent on an annual basis for that quarter—was not enough. Productivity has increased even faster in Western Europe and Japan since 1965 *(see table, p. 7).* The disparity is reflected in the growing inability of American products to compete abroad. The

---

[3] Section 4 of the Economic Stabilization Act Amendment of 1971, signed into law Dec. 22, 1971, is entitled "National Productivity Policy." It states that "it is the policy of the United States to promote efficient production, marketing, distribution, and use of goods and services in the private sector...."

[4] Speech to the National Industrial Conference Board, New York, Jan. 19, 1972. See "Organized Labor After the Freeze," *E.R.R.,* 1971 Vol. II, pp. 823-842.

United States incurred a $2 billion foreign-trade deficit in 1971, its first in this century.

Recent productivity increases are expected to ease inflationary pressures and perhaps reduce or even eliminate a deficit in foreign trade in 1972. But those developments tend to occur only at the expense of continued high unemployment, the most politically sensitive economic problem in this election year. After polling several industries, Ralph E. Winter of *The Wall Street Journal* wrote on March 8, 1972, that "almost all concerns say they will be slow to refill jobs left vacant as a result of cutbacks during the past two years." Winter quoted Glenn Engelke, director of personnel for the Addressograph Corp., as saying that for at least two years, "the name of the game is going to be productivity improvement."

Reasons for Falloff in American Industrial Yields

In some respects, the falloff in productivity can be explained in terms of the business cycle. In the past, output per man-hour behaved in a predictable pattern. It tended to decline at the peak of boom periods—partly because employers were willing to sacrifice efficiency in order to expand production rapidly. Then the decline usually tapered off during recessions as employers looked for ways to cut costs and reduce manpower. And productivity rose quickly in recovery periods. Employers, waiting to see how strong the upturn would be, were usually slow to hire new workers; the existing workers, meanwhile, were producing more than ever to fill the rising demand.

The scenario differed somewhat in the recent recession. For two successive years, 1969 and 1970, productivity growth in the non-farm economy was less than 1 per cent. This was described as "an unusual occurrence in the postwar period" by two economists in the Division of Productivity Research, Bureau of Labor Statistics. [5] Previously, when increases in output per man-hour slowed in one year, they advanced rapidly the next. Several reasons are offered for this two-year decline, including:

A youthful labor force: Young workers are generally considered to be less productive than older, more experienced, workers. During the 1960s the number of workers 16 to 24 years old increased from 12 million to 17 million.

Increase of women workers: Women workers, particularly married women, are generally considered to be less productive

---

[5] Shelby W. Herman and Lawrence J. Fulco, "Changes in Productivity and Unit Labor Costs—A Yearly Review," *Monthly Labor Review*, May 1971, p. 3.

ANNUAL AVERAGE PRODUCTIVITY GAINS,* 1965-70

United States	2.1%	Italy	5.1%
Belgium	6.8	Japan	14.2
Canada	3.5	Netherlands	8.5
France	6.6	Sweden	7.9
Germany	5.3	United Kingdom	3.6

* Per man-hour.
SOURCE: Bureau of Labor Statistics.

---

than men, partly because they take part-time work and because they work at clerical jobs in which productivity is difficult to measure. Seven million women entered the labor force during the past decade, five million of whom were married.

Shift to a service economy: More workers were producing goods than providing services immediately after World War II. But service "industries"—government, transportation, public utilities, trade, finance and real estate—took the lead in the Fifties and this trend accelerated in the Sixties. By 1969, just under 45 million persons in the labor force were providing services while fewer than 25 million were producing goods. Services are generally considered to be less efficient than goods-producing industries.

Arms race and technology lag: Research and development is believed to be a major factor in productivity growth. While the United States made a large expenditure on technology during the Sixties, most of it was concentrated on military and space activities. According to Seymour Melman, professor of industrial engineering and management at Columbia University, the proportion of the gross national product devoted to military purposes (8 to 10 per cent) "includes a preponderance of the research and development, scientific and engineering manpower of the country." The effect of this concentration on military and related work "is the relative technical depletion of many civilian industries and activities." [6]

Emphasis on environmental improvement: While improvement of the environment is necessary and desirable, it can act as a drag on productivity in a strictly economic sense. Money which might be used to increase the productive capacity of the country is now being used to improve the quality of the air, land and water. Since "cleaner air" is not accounted for in calculations of the gross national product or of productivity increases, it represents a loss.

---

[6] Quoted by *The New York Times,* Feb. 6, 1972. See "Technology Lag in America," *E.R.R.,* 1972 Vol. I, pp. 4-6.

Organized labor practices: Unions are frequently accused of contributing to the productivity problem by resisting the introduction of automated equipment, insisting on "featherbedding" and invoking "work to rule" slowdowns.

There are many other reasons suggested for the slowdown in productivity gains. A Brookings Institution economist, Edward F. Denison, believes that a decline in investment for new plant and equipment was a significant factor. George L. Perry, another Brookings economist, believes that unemployment contributed to the productivity crisis. [7] Some observers, however, believe that profound changes in public attitudes had more to do with the productivity problem than purely economic factors.

Rejection of Old Work Ethic on Assembly Line

For one thing, the very idea of economic growth and progress is becoming anathema to an increasing number of Americans. In a *Harvard Business Review* article on the productivity problem, management expert Gordon F. Bloom wrote: "It is unfortunate but true that 'progress' is becoming a bad word in virtually all sectors of our society—conservative, liberal or radical." [8] He and others speculate that this shift in thinking was brought about by the sudden realization of the magnitude of the problems created by pollution, overpopulation and technological advances. Many Americans advocate a national policy of zero economic growth.

While economists cannot measure the impact of this new attitude on productivity, many are convinced that it has contributed to the falloff. Even more important is a basic change in the way young people look at work. "The traditional concept that hard work is a virtue and a duty, which older workers adhere to, is not applicable to younger workers," according to Ken Bannon, a vice president of the United Auto Workers Union. [9]

Corporation executives seem no less puzzled than many other Americans as to why young people entering the labor force—even in a time of job scarcity—are less enchanted with the so-called Protestant ethic of hard work and upward

---

[7] Edward F. Denison, "Comments and Discussion" [on an article by George L. Perry], *Brookings Papers on Economic Activity* (1971).

[8] Gordon F. Bloom (senior lecturer at the Alfred P. Sloan School of Management, Massachusetts Institute of Technology), "Productivity, Weak Link in Our Economy," *Harvard Business Review,* January-February 1971, p. 5.

[9] Letter to Malcolm L. Denise, Ford Motor Co. vice president, made public Feb. 4, 1972.

striking than their parents and grandparents. Even the executive ranks of industry are not entirely free of the new work attitude. University graduates entering business typically profess to abhor aspects of technology that tend to reduce man to a machine-like function. [10]

Worker disaffection has reached what has been termed "crisis" proportions in the automobile industry, but is not confined to that industry. George Meany, president of the AFL-CIO, recently remarked: "There are certain areas in American industry...where you specialize in work doing the same thing. This really does something to workers mentally...They get bored to death, they lose all desire to do anything." [11] The President's Manpower Report of 1969 contained a survey indicating that only 50 to 68 per cent of blue- and white-collar workers felt their work was fulfilling.

Alfred Vogel, vice president in charge of employee relations research at Opinion Research Corporation, wrote that there was "burgeoning discontent" among the 13 million clerical workers in the United States. [12] And an industry study conducted by Harold L. Sheppard of the Upjohn Institute for Employment concluded that "there is no question that job dissatisfaction is increasing." [13] A poll conducted by the Gallup organization in March 1972 indicated that a majority of adult Americans did not believe that workers—themselves included—were producing as much as they should.

Worker Discontent at General Motors Plant

Worker discontent was highly visible at the General Motors complex at Lordstown, Ohio, months before workers struck for 22 days in March 1972 protesting new methods intended to make the assembly line more efficient. The Lordstown plant, which produces Chevrolet Vegas, was consolidated with a nearby Fisher body plant the previous summer. More than 10 per cent of the 8,000 men then on the line were laid off. The workers contended that the company, by reducing the work force, was asking those who remained to work too hard and too fast to turn out quality cars. General

---

[10] See "Changing Corporate World," *E.R.R.*, 1971 Vol. I, pp. 83-88.
[11] Quoted by Haynes Johnson and Nick Kotz in *The Washington Post*, April 11, 1972.
[12] Alfred Vogel, "Your Clerical Workers Are Ripe for Unionism," *Harvard Business Review*, March-April 1971, p. 48.
[13] Quoted by Sam Zagoria, former member of the National Labor Relations Board, in *The Washington Post*, Feb. 6, 1972.

Motors, on the other hand, accused the workers of "shoddy workmanship." The plant was closed down for brief periods several times because defective cars were coming off the line.

The Vega facility is believed to be the fastest-moving assembly line in the world. Each of the workers—whose average age is 24—has only 36 seconds to complete his particular job on any one car. When the strike came, Russell W. Gibbons, a labor editor, wrote that it was "the most dramatic instance of worker resistance since the Flint sit-downs in 1937."

> The issue is not money [he continued], but one which only a few years ago was confined to the philosophical and ideological dialogues of labor educators and seminars on work: the redefinition of work rules and some sort of solution to the dulling, repetitive, and sometimes psychologically killing nature of the assembly line. [14]

"The 'myth of the happy worker'...is still just that," Victor C. Ferkiss wrote in 1969. He noted "alienation from work" particularly at the semi-skilled level. "A basic fact about semi-skilled working-class life: it is on a flat level. There are few differences in pay or responsibility from job to job, from year to year. There is not too much point in working hard to get somewhere for there is no place to go." [15] This basic kind of dissatisfaction—now identified as the "Blue Collar Blues"— has long been considered to be at the root of high rates of labor turnover, absenteeism and tardiness, all of which crucially affect productivity.

Factors in Growth of Productivity

CONCERN OVER PRODUCTIVITY is nothing new in America. Immediately after World War II, the labor movement was under strong pressure to work harder and faster to maintain levels of production reached during the war. Henry Ford II said in 1946 that it was then requiring 128 hours to build a car which in 1941 required only 87 hours. Labor productivity, he said, had gone down 34 per cent while labor costs had doubled. Unions spoke of a "speedup" and argued that productivity was actually increasing. It was difficult to tell be-

---

[14] Russell W. Gibbons, "Showdown at Lordstown," *Commonweal*, March 3, 1972, p. 523.
[15] Victor C. Ferkiss, *Technological Man* (1969), pp. 206, 210. See also "Blue-Collar America," *E.R.R.*, 1970 Vol. II, pp. 635-640.

cause the nearest thing to a productivity measurement was a statistical series provided by the Labor Department on 24 selected manufacturing industries. The Bureau of Labor Statistics reported "no significant change in average productivity" for these industries during the war years but noted a "moderate rise" beginning in 1945. [16]

Only a few years later, the productivity problem was reversed. Leon Keyserling, the chairman of the Council of Economic Advisers in the Truman administration, said "the economy is on the way to being so productive that we won't have large enough outlets for increasing productivity unless new markets are found." At that time, 1950, labor unions were demanding that the gains from higher output per worker be passed on in the form of wage increases. Labor was then beginning to show concern that automation, by reducing the need for workers, might eventually result in massive unemployment.

Productivity became a major labor issue again in the 1960s—this time over voluntary wage-price "guideposts." The guideposts were first enunciated in the 1962 Economic Report of the Council of Economic Advisers. The general guide for wages was that "the percentage increase in total compensation per man-hour be equal to the national trend-rate of increase in output per man-hour." Although the guideposts were unpopular with both business and labor, they produced—in combination with other economic policies—the desired result of holding back inflation until the latter part of the decade. The Johnson administration reacted to rising inflation by exerting new pressure on labor and industry to hold back prices.

President Johnson's "jawbone policy" of exhorting unions and management to stay within explicit guideposts helped to mobilize public opinion but gave rise to new complaints from both sides. By then, the guideposts had been stated in terms of a numerical formula—that wages and prices exceeding 3.2 per cent a year were inflationary. It became increasingly harder to impose the guideposts and toward the end of the Johnson presidency the term "guidepost" had almost disappeared from the political vocabulary.

President Nixon recognizes that productivity is an "often misunderstood" concept. In his 1971 Labor Day address on

---

[16] See "Labor Productivity," *E.R.R.*, 1946 Vol. II, pp. 652-654.

Sept. 6, he said: "That word, productivity, puzzles and some-times frightens people. It sounds like the old 'speed-up' or some new efficiency system that drives people harder." He went on to say that rising output per man-hour means that "the individual worker gets a real increase in wages, and not just a pay raise eaten away by inflation." The trouble is that productivity is easier to define in abstract than in concrete terms.

Long-Term Rise of Productive Efficiency in U.S.

Historically, productivity in American industry increases at a fairly constant rate of between one and two per cent a year, according to Paul A. Samuelson. [17] But there are substantial fluctuations due to war, reconversion to a peacetime economy, automation, changes in the labor force, reductions in the hours of work and other factors. John W. Kendrick, a produc-tivity expert, has calculated that productivity per man-hour increased only 0.8 per cent a year from 1909 to 1929. The yearly increase jumped to 5.8 per cent between 1929 and 1937; many inefficient concerns collapsed in the depression and others were pushed toward mechanization. The annual rate of increase dropped to 1.4 per cent in 1937-47, while the 1948-52 period was marked by spectacular modernization of industry but a less-than-spectacular rise in productivity of about 3 per cent.[18]

Lee A. DuBridge, who was later to become President Nixon's chief science adviser, wrote in 1962:

> The net effect of the gradual increase in productivity means that, with an approximately constant number of man-hours per year—the rising working population being nearly compensated by the decreasing number of hours worked per week—it has been pos-sible to double the output of industrial production every twenty-five to thirty years while the. population has been doubling every forty-five to fifty years. This of course, is the primary source of the increased standard of living which this country has been attaining over the past century. [19]

Agricultural technology, in the form of mechanization, cultivating techniques, fertilizers and insecticides, resulted in a steep rise in farm output per man-hour—and accelerated a decline in farm employment. From 1950 to 1970, this output in agriculture increased by nearly 6 per cent a year. Several

---

[17] Paul A. Samuelson, *Economics* (1955), p. 513.
[18] John W. Kendrick (National Bureau of Economic Research), *Productivity Trends in the United States* (1961).
[19] Lee A. DuBridge, "Educational and Social Consequences," *Automation and Technological Change* (1962), p. 32. Edward E. David Jr. succeeded DuBridge in 1970 as presidential science adviser and as director of the Office of Science and Technology.

U.S. PRODUCTIVITY INCREASES PER MAN-HOUR

Year	Per cent	Year	Per cent
1966	4.0	1969	0.7
1967	2.1	1970	0.9
1968	2.9	1971	3.4

SOURCE: Bureau of Labor Statistics.

---

industries also posted very large productivity gains, but trade and manufacturing, as a whole, fell below 3 per cent. *(See chart on following page.)*

Technological Advances and Shorter Work Hours

Automation is one of the key determinants of productivity increases. Over a period of years automation creates jobs insofar as it spurs economic growth. But automation can lead to heavy unemployment in the short term and to serious displacement of workers within the labor force. Labor responded to automation in a variety of ways but most frequently by trying to block the introduction of automated equipment or by insisting in contract negotiations that management retain redundant employees. The classic example was railroad "featherbedding"—keeping firemen in the cabs even after the abandonment of coal fuel left them with no work to do.

Labor also demanded shorter hours to spread the available work among more workers. [20] The average workweek, estimated to be 70 hours in 1850, dropped to 47.7 hours in the early 1930s and to 40 hours by the early 1940s. The long working day of the Industrial Revolution gave organized labor its first great issue. With the exception of child labor, no other grievance against employers so urgently called for reform as the sunup-to-sundown schedules in factories. Over the years, labor unions never lost interest in fighting for fewer hours of work per week, though their reasons for pressing the issue changed with the times.

In the beginning of the labor movement, it sought simply to relieve workers of the hardship of inhumanly long working days. Toward the end of the 19th century, unions took up the rallying cry for an eight-hour day chiefly as a means of building up strength and winning members. Still later, the demand for a shorter standard workweek became a mechanism for

---

[20] AFL-CIO President George Meany declared in 1963 that the 35-hour week with double pay for overtime work was labor's top goal "to ensure stability and growth." See "Cushioning of Automation," *E.R.R.*, 1963 Vol. II, p. 779.

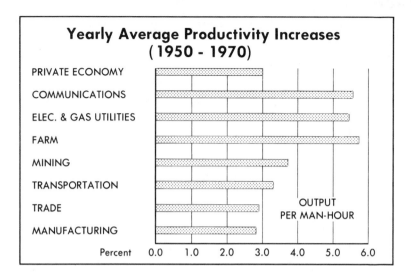

Yearly Average Productivity Increases (1950 - 1970)

PRIVATE ECONOMY
COMMUNICATIONS
ELEC. & GAS UTILITIES
FARM
MINING
TRANSPORTATION
TRADE
MANUFACTURING

OUTPUT PER MAN-HOUR

Percent 0.0 1.0 2.0 3.0 4.0 5.0 6.0

raising wages—by requiring extra pay for hours worked beyond the standard period.

Despite the current interest in productivity and long study of it by economists, there are numerous controversies concerning the way it is measured and used. The productivity index is undoubtedly the most complex of all economic indicators. It reflects the contribution not only of labor but technology, managerial expertise, wealth and natural resources. In a sense, the productivity index is the "bottom line"—net result—of economic performance. Difficulties arise when statisticians try to extrapolate from the over-all index the factors which affected its growth or decline. A frequent criticism is that the index does not show changes in the quality of the goods and services it measures. Herbert Stein, chairman of the Council of Economic Advisers, noted recently that productivity figures do not account for the deterioration of the environment.

> It is obvious that productivity statistics do not measure justice, security, happiness, beauty, or the lack of them, and we cannot be sure in what direction our available measurements may be biased. But this obvious fact does not belie the importance of the statistic as an indication of the ability of society as a whole to achieve its goals. [21]

The most commonly used measure of productivity relates the dollar value of the total output of goods and services to the hours of work required to produce them. At the plant

---

[21] Herbert Stein, "The Meaning of Productivity," *The Meaning and Measurement of Productivity* (Bulletin 1714 of the Bureau of Labor Statistics, 1971), p. 2.

level, the measure is expressed in terms of some physical concept like kilowatt-hours of electricity, tons of steel or barrels of oil per man-hour of work. Economists think of productivity in terms of "input" and output. Input usually consists of labor, capital, material and knowledge. Edward F. Denison has identified some 20 "inputs," including "better allocation of resources," "economies of scale" and "age-sex makeup of the work force."

Labor is stressed in nearly all of these formulas. Labor cost is involved in almost all production, and it is the easiest to measure. But there are several ambiguities in indexes of output per man-hour. Such figures recorded by the Bureau of Labor Statistics [22] generally refer to the time spent at the place of employment and therefore exclude vacation time, illness and tardiness—although these factors may be significant. Nor do the figures take into account standby time, coffee breaks, or idle time resulting from machinery breakdowns. The measurement of productivity is even more difficult in service industries. "In the government sector, the statisticians have to give up and assume no productivity increase at all because they know of no way to estimate one." [23] Government, like most service industries, is "labor intensive"—and labor-intensive industries normally have low levels of productivity.

Directions of Change in Work Scene

THERE ARE SEVERAL trains of thought about the productivity problem in current economic literature. Some writers dispute the idea that a truly serious problem exists. Others believe there is a crisis but that there is little that either government or business can do about it. Peter Drucker wrote that productivity must be increased if inflation is to be managed. Saying that wages must not rise faster than productivity if prices are to remain stable, Drucker concluded:

> The "cost squeeze" of today, on governments, universities, and business, is the first warning—it is really a productivity squeeze. The only way out of it is for the non-manual employee, whether he is a knowledge worker or a policeman, to become more productive.

---

[22] The bureau prepares and publishes quarterly indexes of output per man-hour for the private, farm, non-farm and manufacturing sectors of the economy. Once a year, it publishes indexes of output per man-hour for about 40 selected industries.

[23] "Lower Productivity Threatens Growth," *Business Week,* Jan. 1, 1972, p. 36.

In his own interest, he will find he has to push for this. It is the only way, in the long run, for him to enjoy a comfortable, let alone a rising standard of living.[24]

But it is precisely the idealization of "a rising standard of living" that another group of writers believe may be changing. According to David Anderson of *The Wall Street Journal*: "More people might opt for low pay, less pressure and more free time; they wouldn't be as productive in material terms, but they would be healthier and happier."

> What all of this really implies...[he continued] is that our economy is evolving to a point beyond productivity-fed develop-ment, as currently understood, and that no one can do much about that. But such evolution wouldn't necessarily be calamitous either at home or abroad. If the long-term rate of productivity increase did fall back, say, to the 2.5 per cent range from the cur-rent 3 per cent range, one suspects, we would feel the effects, but no doubt we would consider them worth some of the benefits to the quality of our lives at home.[25]

Predictions of productivity growth over the next five to 10 years vary greatly. So many factors determine productivity that it is difficult, if not impossible, for economists to account for them all. Automation should help productivity, for in-stance, but the continuing shift to a service economy will deter it. Despite these uncertainties, the Council of Economic Advisers estimated that, on the basis of historical trends, output per man-hour would increase at an average rate of 3.1 per cent a year between 1970 and 1975. This forecast made in 1970 is still generally accepted, although an increasing number of economists are questioning it. *Business Week* reported Jan. 1, 1972, that "some economists are already projecting 10-year productivity increases as low as 2.5 per cent annually."

Productivity Bargaining in New Labor Contracts

Sanford Rose of *Fortune* magazine belittles concern over the productivity crisis. He maintains that the business com-munity was largely responsible for the recent decline in pro-ductivity—that it overinvested in plant and equipment, allowed an "unprecedented decline in work discipline" and hoarded labor long after industrial production stopped rising. In his view, work attitudes will improve once management begins to set stiffer labor standards.[26]

---

[24] Peter F. Drucker, "The Surprising Seventies," *Harper's Magazine*, July 1971, p. 39.
[25] David Anderson, *The Wall Street Journal*, Feb. 15, 1972.
[26] Sanford Rose, "The News About Productivity is Better Than You Think," *Fortune*, February 1972.

Productivity and the New Work Ethic

Productivity bargaining has received special attention ever since 1970 when the government began to focus on productivity as the key to better economic performance. Essentially, the new approach involves a tradeoff whereby labor agrees to scrap productivity-inhibiting work rules in exchange for a share of the gains brought about by modernization and increased efficiency. The practice is commonplace in Britain. Jerome M. Rosow, a former Assistant Secretary of Labor (1969-71), credits a labor contract at Fawley, England, with being the first productivity agreement. It was signed in 1960 by the management of an Esso petroleum refinery at Fawley and eight unions representing 6,500 workers.

In return for an easing of union work rules, the workers received wage increases, a reduction in the workweek and safeguards for basic pay. The agreement was "a landmark in British collective bargaining.... It triggered a pattern of reform...throughout much of British industry. It was the harbinger of the theory and practice of productivity bargaining, which was to become a major plank in the National Incomes Policy of the Wilson government."[27]

Robert B. McKersie, dean of the New York School of Industrial Labor Relations, studied the British experience and reported that it had "some useful implications for the United States...[in] longshoring, printing, railroads, airlines and construction." To foster productivity bargaining in this country, McKersie suggested greater planning by management and the education of union leaders "by first-hand observation of successful cases."[28]

A limited form of productivity bargaining is already going on in the United States. A local of the United Rubber Workers in Akron, Ohio, voted in January 1972 to open talks with the B. F. Goodrich Co. on ways to make the Akron plant more productive. At issue is the depression vintage six-hour, six-day workweek instituted by management to spread employment. The company also seeks to cut down a profusion of job classifications which reportedly delayed and increased the cost of maintenance and repairs. For their part, the workers are demanding more job security and more company investment in plant and machinery.

---

[27] Jerome M. Rosow (now an executive of Standard Oil of New Jersey), "Now Is The Time For Productivity Bargaining," *Harvard Business Review*, January-February, 1972, p. 80.

[28] *First Annual Report of the Chairman of the National Commission on Productivity to the President*, March 10, 1971, p. 23.

Productivity bargaining is only one of many ideas suggested by manpower experts. Another is standardization of industrial output. The huge variety of sizes and shapes in shipping cartons retards the handling and loading of shipments. Several European countries are increasing distributive efficiency by getting manufacturers, wholesalers and retailers to agree on the dimensions of their shipping containers.

Incentives to Reduce Absenteeism and Turnover

Manpower experts believe many efforts to improve productivity are doomed to failure if insufficient attention is given to worker attitudes. The division of labor has been the basis of large productivity increases but it has also been the major element in reducing work to a series of boring, repetitive tasks. According to psychoanalyst Erich Fromm, more than economic efficiency is at stake in the effort to improve the interest factor in work. Fromm wrote, "There are good reasons to assume that the increase in boredom is one of the factors responsible for the increase in aggression" in the United States.[29]

Efforts to make employees work harder or more effectively can be traced back to the Thirties when stopwatch-toting efficiency experts clocked the time it took to perform each segment of a job. More recently, managers have reduced work hours, increased benefits and salaries, provided off-hours recreational activities, sponsored vacation trips, and offered prizes, bonuses and a variety of other incentives. Increasingly, however, motivation theory is falling into disrepute. Despite the package of rewards for better work, many of the industries which offer them continue to experience absenteeism, tardiness, defective workmanship and high rates of personnel turnover.

The failure of the classical motivation theory has led to a new emphasis on "job enrichment" as a means of improving worker morale. Robert N. Ford, director for manpower utilization at the American Telephone & Telegraph Co., wrote in 1969: "What we didn't understand adequately was the relationship between employee and customer, not the one between employee and management...."[30] Ford concluded that employees who resist inducements to work harder are not asking to be "recognized" or "treated well" but are asking management to "use me well, let my life mean something."

---

[29] Erich Fromm, "The Erich Fromm Theory of Aggression," *The New York Times Magazine*, Feb. 27, 1972, p. 86.
[30] Robert N. Ford, "The Obstinate Employee," *Psychology Today*, November 1969, p. 33.

Thomas H. Fitzgerald, director of employee research and training activities at the Chevrolet Motor Division of General Motors Corp., has suggested that it may be impossible to motivate workers in any significant way—even with job-restructuring and job-enrichment programs. Fitzgerald argues that people do not want to be motivated, and may consider attempts at it to be an unwarranted intrusion into their lives. "The language of motivation may become subtly elitist by suggesting that the employee resembles a captive rodent in a training box equipped with levers, trick doors, food pellets and electric grids." He also suggests that pervasive "utopian" advertising may have an effect inimical to all efforts to motivate employees.

> The offers of independence, the encouragement to self-aggrandizement and the persistent flattery they experience as audiences all contrast unfavorably with the discipline and the subordination which they experience as employees. Work loses its "religious" character, its centrality as the locus of self.[31]

Despite the complexities of motivational theory, the reward of greater leisure time appears to have increased productivity in some companies. According to a study by the Bureau of Labor Statistics in mid-1971, "about 600" companies were offering some form of the four-day workweek. By early 1972, a study by the American Management Association indicated that 700 to 1,000 companies in the United States and Canada were trying the shorter week. Furthermore, the association said two-thirds of those companies reported a boost in productivity.[32] It is estimated that 75,000 to 100,000 employees, about one worker in a thousand, is on a short workweek. In a few places, the workweek has been shortened to three days— of 12-hour shifts.

Industry's Experiments With Four-Day Workweek

According to economist Janice Neipert Hedges, the movement toward fewer work days is in accord with two other trends. The first is the preference for blocks of leisure time— extended vacations, for example—rather than small reductions in daily and weekly work hours. The second is in an increasing diversity in work schedules.[33] Several firms are reported to be experimenting with a "gliding workday" in

---

[31] Thomas H. Fitzgerald, "Why Motivation Theory Doesn't Work," *Harvard Business Review*, July-August 1971, p. 40.

[32] "Latest on the Four-Day Week," *U.S. News & World Report*, Feb. 20, 1972. See also "Four-Day Week," *E.R.R.*, 1971 Vol. II, pp. 609-626.

[33] Janice Neipert Hedges, "A Look at the 4-Day Workweek," *Monthly Labor Review*, October 1971, p. 34.

which workers set their own arrival and departure time within a 12-hour period.

Some manpower experts think that productivity gains resulting from new work scheduling will be short-lived. While the switch to four days may help a company hire experienced (and productive) workers today, the advantage is likely to be lost when its competitors adopt the same practice. Moreover, not all workers like the changeover. And those who like it now may find the longer daily hours—which most short-week schedules require—will soon become a drag. In that case, management can again expect absenteeism, tardiness and turnover.

Persuasive arguments are being marshalled on all sides of the productivity question: whether it is serious, whether it can be solved, and whether the goal is worthwhile. As has happened several times in the past, efficient production is once again being put forward as the key to national economic health. But what is new this time is the implied challenge of the new work ethic—a challenge to the very premise that greater productivity is necessarily good.

FOUR-DAY WEEK

by

Helen B. Shaffer

1 9 7 1
Aug. 11

FOUR-DAY WEEK

HUNDREDS OF AMERICAN firms have recently converted some or all of their work schedules to a four-day week, many more small companies are expected to follow suit soon, and pressures for a four-day week are rising in two major industries—automobile and steel production. As a result, enthusiasts for the changeover are hailing the four-day week as the workweek of the future. Some do not stop there, but view the four-day week as a mere way station on the road to a three-day week. A few companies have, in fact, already instituted this dream week in which there are more days to play than days to work.

Workweek watchers differ in their estimates of the strength or pace of the movement toward fewer workdays. But none denies that interest is mounting rapidly. Employers, workers, and government officials are all taking particular notice of a movement that seems to have sprung suddenly out of nowhere. Labor union leaders are interested, too, though chary of a return to the long workday of the sweatshop era, even if the worker is compensated with an extra day off each week.

Whether or not the four-day week will ultimately prevail as the norm for the nation, recent developments in work scheduling are significant, for they are symptomatic of a breakaway from the fixed pattern of Monday-Friday work which governs the life of nearly all Americans. Numerous different new combinations of worktime are being tried out to fit the needs of individual companies or to please particular groups of workers. "All the attention and publicity generated by workweek innovations indicate that changes in work patterns are in the offing," *Business Week* commented. Among the changes from the prevailing standard, a workweek of four 9- or 10-hour days appears to be the favored plan at this time. The magazine noted further that "the novelty of a shorter workweek coupled with glowing testimonials from the participants is forcing management to take a look whether it is ready or not."[1]

The great boon of the four-day week is, of course, the long free weekend. Its great drawback is the lengthened workday. However, the long-day, short-week plan could lead in due time to a short-day, short-week plan. But even before that halcyon era arrives, a spread of the four-day week could have far-reaching effects on the American life style. For some, especially older, job-oriented workers, there may be a problem of what to do with the long weekends. But there are signs that the work ethic does not hold as strong a grip on young people.[2] So it may be that the three-day or four-day weekend is due to arrive in the nick of time.

Many changes, both personal and institutional, are likely to occur, but at this time most of them are quite conjectural. What, for instance, will a four-day schedule do to the traffic burden of a large city? Will the reduced number of workdays lessen congestion—or will Monday-to-Thursday rush hours merely grow longer? A hundred similar questions will remain unanswered with any degree of certainty until the shorter work-week becomes widespread enough to provide a body of experience.

Business Interest in Reports About Rescheduling

Interest in the four-day week surged with the publication in November 1970 of *4 days, 40 hours: Reporting a Revolution in Work and Leisure,* a symposium reporting on various aspects of the movement. Most of the chapters are keyed to an account by the book's editor and publisher, Riva Poor, on her investigation of 27 companies that had tried some variant of the shorter week. Nearly all of the companies had initiated a four-day week no earlier than 1969.

Mrs. Poor, a 35-year-old management consultant at Cambridge, Mass., concluded from these studies that "the four-day, 40-hour workweek is spreading in our society—and spreading rapidly." So certain was she that many more concerns would like to leap on the 4-40 bandwagon, she put the book together within a few months in the hope that it would serve as a guidance manual for an effective and profitable changeover. Her interest was sparked in May 1970 when she

---

[1] "Why the Work Week Pattern is Changing," *Business Week,* March 13, 1971, p. 108.
[2] See "Changing Corporate World," *E.R.R.,* 1971 Vol. I, pp. 83-88.

discovered a company reaping a clear gain from the change-over. Fascinated by the novelty of the idea, she and her aides began searching for other worktime innovators.

By the time the book was ready for publication, they had found some three dozen four-day concerns with a total of 7,000 employees and a few three-day companies too. Since then Mrs. Poor and her associates have continued their search with a view to publishing more reports of work schedule revisions. As of August 1971, they had discovered about 500 companies that had drastically revised workweek schedules for at least some of their employees. These companies were located in 46 states; California, Florida, Indiana, Massachusetts, Minnesota, North Carolina, New Jersey, New York, Oregon, Pennsylvania, and Texas accounted for a majority of them. Early growth had been in the East, but there was a recent spurt in the central states. And the rate of conversions had apparently increased nationally, from an average of one company converting every three days in the fall of 1970 to a rate of three every day by midsummer 1971.

The book caught on quickly and apparently inspired a number of firms to try a new work schedule. Mrs. Poor told Editorial Research Reports that it had sold 43,000 copies by early August 1971, including sales abroad, and had been the subject of 1,500 articles in the general and trade press. At the request of the American Management Association, she had served as chairman of a seminar on the four-day week. So many inquiries were received, Mrs. Poor said, she started publishing a newsletter.

Government Studies of Short-Week Innovations

Publicity about companies that have succeeded with the innovation has helped spread the movement. Kyanize Paints, Inc., a small manufacturer in Everett, Mass., upon being described in several trade journals as having pioneered the four-day movement, reported that it had received more than 1,200 requests for information on how it is making out since it instituted the change in 1969.[3] Kenneth E. Wheeler, a management consultant at Lowell, Mass., received inquiries from 300 to 400 companies after the *Harvard Business Review* published an article he wrote on the four-day week for small business.[4]

---

[3] "Why the Workweek Pattern is Changing," *Business Week*, March 13, 1971, p. 108.

[4] Kenneth E. Wheeler, "Small business eyes the four-day workweek," *Harvard Business Review*, May-June 1970, p. 142.

The Labor Department has received a flurry of inquiries from companies wanting to know how going on a four-day week would affect their situation under statutory wage-hour provisions covering government contract work. Federal law provides that employers doing business with the government must pay extra wages for work beyond eight hours a day even if the weekly total does not exceed 40. The companies were informed there is no way of evading this requirement. But the department will hold hearings, beginning Sept. 7, 1971, on whether to recommend that existing law be changed to accommodate those employers and employees who prefer a 4-40 to a 5-40 schedule.[5] Sen. Marlow W. Cook (R Ky.) introduced a bill Aug. 6, 1971, to so change the law.

The Civil Service Commission found interest in four-day work sufficiently strong among federal employees that in the spring of 1971 it initiated a study of its possibilities in government service. "There is no thought of closing down government offices three days a week," a Civil Service spokesman told Editorial Research Reports. "The movement is in the other direction," he said. "We are thinking of trying to improve service, possibly with two shifts of workers to keep government offices open six days a week." If the results of the study are favorable to the movement, the commission's next step would be to draw up suggestions for four-day week tryouts among selected groups of employees. These suggestions would be submitted to heads of the various government departments. As in the case of government contract work, any change toward adopting a four-day week would require congressional action to avoid overtime pay.

While the federal government has pondered, several city governments have acted. Policemen in Huntington Beach, Calif., started working a four-day week in May 1969 and since then the practice has spread. The police department in nearby Long Beach adopted it early in 1971 and some units in Memphis and Washington, D.C., have been placed on four-day schedules. All but a few municipal employees in the Minneapolis suburb of Minnetonka shifted in July 1971 to the four-day week and in the same month Atlanta began testing this scheduling for some city workers.

---

[5] The major federal laws applying the eight-hour standard to work under government contract are the Davis-Bacon Act of 1931, the Walsh-Healey Public Contracts Act of 1936, and the Work Hours Act of 1962. These acts differ from the Fair Labor Standards Act of 1938, which applies generally to private employment engaged in interstate commerce and imposes a 40-hour-week standard without regard to the number of hours worked daily. *See pp. 617-618.*

The four-day workweek has, surprisingly enough, been largely employer-initiated and it has been instituted mainly in small firms. On both of these counts, however, developments in recent months indicate a broadening of the movement. The big labor unions are coming forward on the four-day week issue, partly in response to worker interest, partly in an effort to protect labor's position if basic schedule changes are going to be made. And major industries as well as small business operators are now hearkening to the claims that a four-day week can reduce costs or boost output.

Experiments by Big Corporations and Big Unions

Chrysler Corp. and the United Automobile Workers have decided to study the feasibility of trying a four-day, 40-hour week schedule for some of the company's production and maintenance workers. This decision became part of a collective bargaining agreement reached Jan. 19, 1971, by Chrysler and the union. No provision of this kind was written into contracts the UAW previously signed with Ford Motor Co. and General Motors Corp. The first suggestion that the four-day week in auto plants be studied came from UAW Vice-President Douglas Fraser, director of the union's Chrysler department, during a discussion between negotiators about absenteeism and labor turnover, both extremely vexing problems in the automobile industry.

The Detroit correspondent of *Iron Age* described the study project as a "UAW trial balloon," adding that the "union's track record with trial balloons makes it necessary to take a serious look at the question."[6] The reference was to the auto union's past successes in pioneering such innovations in collective bargaining as health insurance, pension plans, cost-of-living increases, and a guaranteed annual wage. An official of the National Association of Manufacturers saw the Chrysler study as indicative of a new outlook on the part of management toward the shorter week. "Until a year and a half ago," said Mrs. Phyllis Moehrle, assistant to the NAM vice-president for industrial relations, "we had the impression company management would resist the four-day week. But the growing number of small companies that are adopting it and...[the] expression of interest by Chrysler indicate there is a desire to experiment."[7]

---

[6] "The Sabbath Day Grows Longer," *Iron Age*, Jan. 28, 1971, p. 36.
[7] Quoted in *Industry Week*, Feb. 1, 1971, p. 11.

The United Steelworkers of America, which for several years has been pressing for a shorter workweek both through legislation and collective bargaining, spoke approvingly at its 1970 convention of current switches to the four-day week. "Employers who have experimented with the four-day week are highly pleased," a report of the union's officers stated. "They are discovering that happier, less tired workers can produce more and better goods."[8] The Steelworkers are plumping for a workweek of four eight-hour days and are not likely to warm up to a 4-40 plan. Union President I.W. Abel told the Steelworkers' convention in 1969 that he aimed to have all union members on a four-day week by 1974.

There is other evidence of increased initiative on the part of labor in what began as an employer-inspired thing. Nearly 15 per cent of the four-day-week companies counted by Mrs. Poor were unionized. "The trend has changed," *Poor's Workweek Letter* reported in its first issue, July 1, 1971. Locals that have sought or agreed to significant schedule changes, chiefly to a four-day week, belong to major international bodies representing machinists, teamsters, and electrical, oil-chemical-atomic, rubber, service, and wood workers. Armour & Co. negotiated a contract in January 1971 with a Teamster local that put 250 employees at a frozen-food plant in Fairmont, Minn., on a 4-40 shift and "indicated it was interested in negotiating similar changes at other plants."[9]

Workweek Reform: Past and Present

THE BOOK OF GENESIS provided the western world with its earliest justification for the idea that days of work should be regularly separated by a day of rest. The example set by the Deity in the act of creation has remained the basic model for man to this day. The five-day and now the four-day or three-day week are merely extensions from the biblical model. The ancient Jews' strict enforcement of the Sabbath, as the terms were set forth in the Third Commandment, emphasized its significance not only as a day of religious devotions, but

---

[8] United Steelworkers of America, *Report of Officers, 15th Constitutional Convention* (Atlantic City, N.J., Sept. 8 - Oct. 2, 1970), p. 13.

[9] "Four-day workweek," *Monthly Labor Review* (Department of Labor publication), May 1971, p. 78.

as a day in which all forms of labor, such as performed during the other days of the week, were strictly forbidden.

Sunday took on a similarly separate character under Constantine, the first Christian emperor, and the church in succeeding centuries sustained the concept of the Lord's Day as one of rest from the week's toil. The importance of observing the Lord's Day to America's Puritan forefathers is well known. Sunday may not have been much fun under their stern theocratic rule, but no child growing up in a Puritan household could mistake Sunday for a workday.

The concept of Sunday as a non-working day has persisted into a secular era. The once-prevalent Blue Laws, forbidding commercial activity on Sunday, were originally inspired by piety. But even as the secular spirit became dominant in the United States, the desire to protect workers from exploitation helped to sustain these laws in many localities.[10] Antipathy to working on Sunday is so ingrained in the American consciousness that many union contracts call for higher pay for working that day than any other.

Early Struggle to Cut Hours of Work Per Day

Most of labor's great gains in reducing hours of work over the past century were obtained by cutting back the hours of the workday rather than cutting back the number of days worked. Even as the average workweek in industry declined from an estimated 69.7 hours in 1850 to 47.7 hours in 1930, the six-day week prevailed. Many younger American workers may not realize how recently the five-day week became prevalent. "The first known five-day week appeared in the United States as recently as 1908, and was unique for years. A decade later, in 1918, there were only a handful of five-day firms. And in 1929 only 5 per cent of the American labor force was on five-day."[11] It was not until the 1930s that the 5½-day and then the five-day week became the norm.

There was a historic reason for labor's emphasis on the length of the day, rather than the number of workdays. The long working day of the early years of the industrial revolution gave labor its first great issue. Of all grievances against employers at that time, none so urgently called for reform as the sunup-

---

[10] See "Sunday Selling," *E.R.R.*, 1960 Vol. I, pp. 119-136.

[11] Riva Poor, "Reporting a Revolution in Work and Leisure: 27 Four-Day Firms," *4 days, 40 hours* (1970), p. 17.

to-sundown schedules in the factories. "In effect, the progress toward a shorter workday and a shorter workweek is a history of the labor movement itself," AFL-CIO President George Meany once told a labor conference.[12] In retrospect, it can be seen that the struggle for shorter workdays was a prelude to the movement from a six-day to a five-day week.

Over the years, labor unions never lost interest in fighting for fewer hours of work per week, though their reasons for pressing the issue changed with the times. In the beginning labor sought simply to relieve workers of the hardship of the inhumanly long working day. Toward the end of the 19th century, unions took up the rallying cry for an eight-hour day as a means of building up strength and winning members. Still later the demand for a shorter standard workweek became a mechanism for raising wages—by requiring premium pay for working longer than the standard period.

The first national effort to put economic pressure on employers for an eight-hour day was directed by the Federation of Organized Trades and Labor Unions, a predecessor of the American Federation of Labor, which set May 1, 1886, as a day of general strike for this goal. Several hundred thousand workers participated in the work stoppage, but the Haymarket Square riot three days later discredited the movement.[13] The American Federation of Labor, first organized under that name in December 1886, was dedicated from the start to the eight-hour day. It adopted a strategy of giving all-out support to each union in turn that took up the fight. "From 1886 to 1890 ...the hours-of-work movement...even more than wage issues, converted the unions into practical, hard-hitting organizations dedicated to the improvement of conditions for workers on the job."[14] The strategy worked, first for the carpenters, then for the miners, the bakers, and typographers.

Long hours continued to prevail in most private employment, however. The steel industry, manned largely by immigrant labor, did not give up the 12-hour day until 1923. By the end of the 1920s, however, organized labor had generally achieved

---

[12] His remarks are found in *The Shorter Work Week* (papers given at a conference on shorter hours of work, sponsored by the AFL-CIO, Sept. 11, 1956), p. 4.

[13] The riot occurred after a bomb exploded during a demonstration for the eight-hour day at Haymarket Square, Chicago, on May 4, 1886. Seven policemen and four others were killed and 100 wounded. Eight anarchists were tried for inciting the riot; four were hanged, one committed suicide, and the remaining three were pardoned by Gov. John Peter Altgeld of Illinois in 1893 on the ground that their trial had been unjust.

[14] George Brooks, "Historical Background," *The Shorter Work Week* (1957), p. 12.

the eight-hour day with a Saturday half-holiday. Building trade unions—painters and plasterers mainly—and workers in unionized manufacturing had won a five-day week by this time, but the workweek for the latter group exceeded 40 hours. On the eve of the Depression Thirties, the average production worker in manufacturing put in 44 hours a week. The average for other workers, however, was close to 48 hours.

During the depression, the short-week campaign became a share-the-work movement, generated largely by craft unions seeking to protect their members. With millions out of work and the economy in a bad way, many unions called for a 30-hour week and bills were introduced in Congress to require it. Work-sharing programs were put into effect in some plants, but they usually entailed loss of pay for those working the shorter hours.

Fixing of 5-Day, 40-Hour Standard in Thirties

A 30-hour bill sponsored by Sen. Hugo L. Black (D Ala.), now a Supreme Court justice, passed the Senate by a vote of 53 to 30 on April 9, 1933, and won House committee approval. But it dropped from sight when interest shifted to the National Recovery Act, which was enacted that year as a major instrument for fighting the depression. The act did not establish a standard workweek but provided for cooperative action by business, labor, and government to establish codes for different industries. Most of the codes specified a 40-hour week. When the Supreme Court invalidated the act in 1935, the average number of hours worked in manufacturing had declined to 36.5.

Other acts of Congress in that decade were instrumental in making the 40-hour week the national norm. As a forerunner, the Davis-Bacon Act of 1931 required companies doing construction work for the government to pay their workers overtime rates beyond eight hours a day but made no provision for work in excess of 40 hours a week. [15] The Walsh-Healey Act of 1936 imposed both an eight-hour day and a 40-hour-week standard on companies holding government supply contracts of $10,000 or more. The Fair Labor Standards Act of 1938 applied a 44-hour (later 40) standard—but no daily standard— to millions of workers in private business who engaged in interstate commerce or made goods sold in interstate commerce—that is, sold outside their state.

---

[15] Those workers had to await passage of the Work Hours Act of 1962 to receive 40-hour protection. Until then, they could be worked eight hours a day for seven days a week without receiving overtime-pay benefits.

Labor unions, including the new industrial unions which were then in their period of great growth, tended to follow the statutory model. But even when unions succeeded in negotiating a workweek shorter than 40 hours, the new schedule almost invariably called for shorter rather than fewer workdays. When rubber workers in 1936 won a 30-hour week, for example, the work was spread over six days. The wage-hour provisions of the Fair Labor Standards Act were intended to attain the law's objective of eliminating "labor conditions detrimental to the maintenance of the minimum standard of living necessary for the health, efficiency, and general well-being of workers." The overtime pay requirement was viewed as a penalty on employers who went beyond the statutory standard and as an incentive to employ more workers.

Labor's Recurring Demands for 30-Hour Week

With the economy going into a boom as entry into World War II neared, the original purpose of the measure became obscured. The hours-of-work standard tended to be regarded as a means of added income for workers who preferred to work more than 40 hours at higher rates. At the peak of war production in 1945, the average workweek reached 45½ hours; President Roosevelt in February 1943 had ordered a 48-hour week in labor shortage areas and many war workers actually put in many more than 48 hours a week. When war orders were cut back, labor revived its call for a 30-hour week. A number of 30-hour bills were introduced in Congress. But the anticipated unemployment did not occur after the war and the unions turned instead to other goals—higher wages and various fringe benefits.

A resurgence of interest in reducing the workweek occurred in the 1950s, largely as a result of union concern over the imminence of technological unemployment.[16] The American Federation of Labor voted at its 1953 convention to "press vigilantly" toward the 30-hour goal. At the convention that united the two major labor federations in December 1955, the AFL-CIO adopted resolutions calling for shortening the standard 40-hour workweek both through legislation and by collective bargaining. In the same year the United Automobile Workers voted to "place the winning of the shorter workweek at the top of our union's collective bargaining agenda after the guaranteed wage has been achieved."

---

[16] See "Four-Day Week," *E.R.R.*, 1957 Vol. I, pp. 345-362, and "Automation and Jobs," *E.R.R.*, 1959 Vol. I, pp. 403-420.

Among major unions that went on record in 1955-57 pledging to press for a shorter workweek were the International Association of Machinists, the Textile Workers Union, International Brotherhood of Electrical Workers, the Communications Workers Union, and the United Steelworkers. Some reduction in worktime was gained through these efforts. The five-day week, however, remained the standard. The four-day week was not unknown, but it was utilized only in special cases—for certain truckdrivers, for example—and until recently almost no effort was made to promote it as a suitable norm for the nation.

In Britain, too, trade-union demands for fewer working hours are beginning to be voiced in terms of a four-day week. The London *Daily Mail,* a pro-Conservative daily, said in a recent editorial on a union's attempt to institute a 35-hour workweek: "This is not quite as pie-in-the-sky as it sounds. In the United States where they're several computer years ahead of us, the four-day working week is already catching on. And there's no reason why it shouldn't catch on here."

Benefits and Drawbacks of Changeover

EMPLOYERS WHO TOOK the initiative in introducing the four-day week did so for good reason: they expected to benefit from it. And most of them—though not all—did. Most of their employees were pleased too and the contentment is another plus for management. The argument for the four-day week was succinctly presented in the May 1, 1971, issue of *Forbes,* the business magazine. An editorial, which occupied an entire page of the magazine in poster style, stated in its entirety:

HOW TO END UNEMPLOYMENT
AND ENSURE RENEWED PROSPERITY
FOR MANY YEARS TO COME
Institute the four-day Work Week

A few weeks later *Forbes* disclosed that it planned to place all of its 250 employees, then on a five-day, 37-hour week, on a four-day, 36-hour week by the end of 1971. Employees will have every Friday off. Company President Malcolm S. Forbes said he expected the change to "present certain problems, but I think they are solvable."[17]

Humanist reformers a century ago argued that a rested and refreshed worker made a better worker—and a better customer too. When Henry Ford in the early 1920s decided to put his men on a five-day week, he said: "We believe that in order to live properly, every man should have more time to spend with his family." Ford was also upholding the theory that a working class with leisure was necessary if an economically viable balance between production and consumption was to be obtained. This viewpoint gained some adherents in the business community during the 1920s. A President's Committee on Recent Economic Changes stated in a 1929 report that American business was coming to realize "in a practical way... not only that leisure is 'consumable' but that people cannot 'consume' leisure without consuming goods and services, and that leisure which results from an increased man-hour productivity helps to create new needs and new and broader markets."[18]

A direct application of this theory was seen in 1971 when Wright and McGill Co., a Denver, Colo., manufacturer of fishing tackle, decided to put its 550 employees on a 37-hour Monday-through-Thursday schedule, with pay for 40 hours. The company said it had made the change because "people who make leisure products should be leaders in providing more leisure time."[19]

Revision of Schedules to Improve Productivity

Over the long haul, a decrease in worktime with no loss of pay is made possible by increased productivity. As productivity increased, labor sought and won a share of the gains in the form of higher wages and more time off. In the case of the four-day week, however, employers have sought it in order to improve productivity by introducing more efficient scheduling. In many cases, the output has increased with a shorter work schedule. In some cases, costly problems of absenteeism and rapid labor turnover have been overcome.

One way of increasing productivity is by more intensive use of equipment during an extended day. This could be true in a

---

[17] Quoted in *The Wall Street Journal,* June 9, 1971.

[18] Cited in "Hours of Labor," *Encyclopedia of the Social Sciences,* Vol. IV, p. 478.

[19] "Four-day workweek," *Monthly Labor Review,* May 1971, p. 77.

manufacturing plant that operates by producing its product in batches. A paint company, for example, found it could produce more during a four-day 36-hour week than it did during its previous five-day 40-hour week. This was because it could produce only three batches of paint on the eight-hour day but could produce four batches during a nine-hour day.

There is almost no end to the varieties of arrangements by which companies have sought to revise work schedules to improve their economic situation. Some plans cut across traditional objections to Sunday work. A chain of retail tire stores in California went on a four-day schedule on a Thursday-through-Sunday basis because their business is best those days.

One of the oldest four-day systems, dating back about 30 years, has applied to certain drivers of oil and gasoline delivery trucks. After considerable experimentation, oil companies settled on the four-day plan as well suited to a round-the-clock operation. The men drive 10-hour shifts, alternating four days on and four days off.

Among businesses shifting to the shorter week, some operate four days a week; others remain open five, giving some workers Monday off, others Friday. One company keeps only an emergency staff on duty Fridays. Still others have found it advantageous to keep production workers on a Monday-through-Thursday schedule, leaving Friday for maintenance and repairs, thus saving by not having to pay overtime for the latter on Saturdays. A mail-service firm in Washington, D.C., converted to a 4-40 plan with shifts arranged so that its 80 employees get a five-day weekend every third week.

Two insurance companies have put selected employees on a three-day week. Metropolitan Life in New York has 500 of its data-processing employees working 12-hour shifts three days a week; Mutual of New York worked out a similar plan (12½ hours a day) for about 40 operators in its computer room in Syracuse, N.Y. The reason at both companies is the same: to get the maximum use out of expensive rented equipment.

A Boston harpsichord maker put his workers on a three-day week because he wanted more leisure time himself. European Health Spa, with 94 branches and 3,000 employees, found the three-day schedule worked out fine because it permitted dividing up the week into three days for male employees and clientele and three days for female. Its three-day plan has been in use nearly 20 years. Perhaps the oddest new schedule is provided for laboratory workers at Latter-Day Saints Hospital in Salt Lake City. They work seven 10-hour days one week, then have the next week off. The 70-hour week would be prohibitively expensive for any company subject to the 40-hour rule of the Fair Labor Standards Act.

Four-Day Week as Way to Counter Absenteeism

A major goal of employers who have gone over to fewer days of work has been simply to please their employees. This is particularly true where there is absenteeism, labor turnover and difficulty of recruitment. The first two problems induced Chrysler and the auto union to take on the study of the four-day week. Absenteeism at all the major automobile plants is estimated to be twice as high as 10 years ago; on some Mondays and Fridays, 20 per cent of the workers fail to show up. Absenteeism is particularly disruptive on assembly lines; the absent worker's replacement is often an inexperienced substitute.

Some managers feel that since so many workers are already taking an unauthorized three-day weekend, it might be wise to make production schedules conform. In some cases, companies have reinforced the new system by paying four-day, 36-hour workers for 40 hours if there is no tardiness or absenteeism in the week. In some cases, employees have agreed to a shortened lunch period and fewer coffee breaks to compensate for the reduced workweek.

Absenteeism was much in mind when business organizations, among others, persuaded Congress in 1968 to shift the observance of three public holidays to Monday,[20] beginning in 1971. The Chamber of Commerce and the National Association of Manufacturers joined with a number of unions, the U.S. Budget Bureau, the Civil Service Commission and the departments of Commerce and Labor in arguing for long holiday weekends in preference to a single-day holiday falling in mid-week. Business spokesmen testified in committee hearings that absenteeism was high before and after a mid-week holiday.

Concern over the declining rate of productivity increases has helped stimulate interest in the four-day week. Productivity gains averaged less than one per cent in 1969 and 1970, com-

---

[20] Washington's Birthday (Feb. 22) to be observed on the third Monday in February; Memorial Day (May 30) to be observed the last Mondays in May; and Veterans Day (Nov. 11) to be observed the fourth Monday in October. The same legislation established Columbus day as a national holiday, to be celebrated the second Monday in October. Labor Day, traditionally observed the first Monday in September, makes the fifth Monday holiday of the year.

pared with average annual gains since World War II of more than 3 per cent. There is a growing suspicion that worker attitude has something to do with the decline. "The...possibility must be confronted," *Fortune* observed recently, "that some profound new difficulty is impairing productivity....If new factors are indeed sapping productivity, they may be social in character, having to do, for example, with the effects of affluence, the youth scene, and expanded welfare upon attitudes toward work." In an earlier issue, the magazine explored the problem of dissatisfaction among younger workers in automobile plants.[21] These workers were said to be "restless, changeable, mobile, demanding, all traits that make for impermanence—and for difficult adjustment to an assembly line." The men frankly disliked the job and couldn't wait to "stampede out the plant gate to the parking lots."

Managers in diverse occupations complain of employee inefficiency due to indifference and lack of commitment to the job. "With all respect to U.S. industry," Kenneth Wheeler observed, "we really are not very efficient. A majority of managers acknowledge that plant and clerical labor operate at between 50 per cent and 60 per cent of their potential." A study of discontented blue-collar workers notes that "there is a prevalent feeling that something has gone wrong for many lower-middle-class Americans." The author was referring to "bored and angry blue-collar workers" found usually on dull, repetitive, dead-end jobs.[22]

The owner of an assembly-line plant, who had found it difficult to recruit good workers because the work was boring and the plant was located in a rural area without public transportation, told a reporter that switching to a four-day, 36-hour week had helped solve his problems and that he was now getting "five days' work out of four days." "The whole thing is attitude," he said. "This four-day week has changed the attitude of people. We communicate better, help each other more. It's just created harmonious working conditions."[23]

Should the four-day week become general, some of the competitive advantages in recruiting and holding good workers

---

[21] See "A Poor Performance in Productivity," *Fortune*, April 1971, p. 18, and Judson Gooding, "Blue-Collar Blues on the Assembly Line," *Fortune*, July 1970, p. 69. See also "Blue-Collar America," *E.R.R.*, 1970 Vol. II, pp. 638-640.

[22] Harold L. Sheppard, "Discontented blue-collar workers—a case study," *Monthly Labor Review*, April 1971, p. 25.

[23] Quoted by Gertrude Samuels in "Thank God It's Thursday! Coming Soon? The Four Day Week," *New York Times Magazine*, May 16, 1971.

would be lost. There is also a suspicion that the novelty is appealing but that in time the good effects will wear off. And there are some employers who have tried the four-day week and given it up, usually because it did not produce the great gains in productivity and worker morale they had anticipated. Or they found that their customers expected service the full week. In other cases the technical problems of working out a smooth operation on the new plan were overwhelming.

Problems and Complaints Involved in Short Week

Women workers present a special problem, especially where there is state or local regulation of female employment. At least two states—Oklahoma and Wisconsin—have modified their laws protective of women workers to ease the change to a four-day 40-hour week. Some women welcome the extra day in which to shop or do other domestic chores. But mothers of young children may have problems with baby sitters or want to go home soon after their children return from school.[24] And there is no move afoot to eliminate Monday or Friday from the school week. Male workers have been heard to complain that being off work Friday merely subjects them to domestic chores they would otherwise miss. Fathers in the home on Mondays or Fridays are also available for becoming involved in the school affairs of their children, such as consulting with teachers over report cards and behavior problems.

The extra day off is expected to encourage workers to take long weekend trips or live farther from their places of employment. Millard C. Faught, a promoter of the three-day week as a national ideal, has suggested that the jobholder will be emancipated from his enslavement to "Megalopolis." The worker, in this vision of the future, would commute to work only once a week, probably in a car pool. He and his fellows would rent an apartment or "barracks facility" where they would sleep two nights a week (between their three work-days); the rest of their time would be spent continuously with their families.

> I envisage [he added] a veritable resurgence of all the traditional self-help and group-help patterns of frontier life out there on those new frontiers in Hinterlurbia, when these four-day-weekend pioneers get there. And the market impact for everything from hand tools to pickup trucks will be reverberative....Give man some real time to use

---

[24] Nearly 26 million children under 18 had mothers in the labor force, according to a Labor Department survey in March 1970. Nearly six million of the children were under six years old.

his tools, and some room, and...all those Yankee craftmanship traditions, skills, and incentives will reflower in a time-wealthy world.[25]

Perhaps the best the four-day week offers at this time is what economist Paul A. Samuelson has foreseen for it: a wider choice of options for the ordinary man, to work long or short hours as he wishes. This is "an area where modern man has had the fewest personal options," he pointed out. As it is, "If other people work nine to five, then you must conform at the peril of being denied your daily bread."[26] While unquestionably many persons on a short workweek would choose to hold two jobs[27] in a future of ample job opportunity, working long hours for extra pay would be a socially acceptable option. Whether or not the four-day week or the three-day week becomes the norm, there will always be some for whom even the seven-day week is not enough.

B. F. Skinner, the Harvard psychologist, envisioned as far back as 1948 in his utopian *Walden Two* the need for no more than four hours of labor a day to keep a model community fed and satisfied. Skinner foresaw a community where leisure time was spent wisely and well. But American workmen have traditionally shown no knack for what Paul Goodman calls "serious leisure." Herman Kahn and Anthony J. Siener of the Hudson Institute "think tank" project that by the end of the century the average lower- middle-class worker will be earning $10,000 to $20,000 (in terms of 1965 dollars) in a year of brief workweeks but "might still wish to increase income by moonlighting or by the wife's working."

There can be no doubt that the four-day week is beginning to catch on. And it will probably catch on a lot more if current moves to revise wage-hour legislation succeed. For labor the move to a 4-40 schedule means a wrenching break with the past. Labor's historic struggle for economic power in America is so enmeshed in the fight for the eight-hour day that it is hard for the old guard particularly to accept a return to the 10-hour day. It is taken for granted that if the big unions accept a 4-40 plan it will be with the idea of using it as a wedge toward cutting back the workweek.

---

[25] Millard C. Faught, "The 3-Day Revolution to Come" in *4 days, 40 hours,* p. 139.

[26] See Samuelson's introduction to *4 days, 40 hours* and his column in *Newsweek,* Nov. 16, 1970, p. 91.

[27] Between three and four millions, or from 4.5 to 5.7 per cent of the labor force, are currently moonlighting.—Vera C. Perrella, "Moonlighters: their motivations and characteristics," *Monthly Labor Review,* August 1970, p. 57.

However it goes, the three-day weekend appears to be the weekend of the future. It is already available to millions of workers at least five times a year because of celebrating five national holidays on Monday. But the trend may not stop there. Those few companies that have already instituted the dream week of more days to play than work may indeed be the pace-setters of the future.

BLUE-COLLAR AMERICA

by

Helen B. Shaffer

1 9 7 0
Aug. 26

BLUE-COLLAR AMERICA

A MAJOR COMPONENT of the Nixon administration's "silent majority" has turned out to be an old friend of the Democrats: the blue-collar worker. Recent demonstrations of "hard hat" support for President Nixon and his policies on the Viet Nam War gave cheering evidence to the Republicans that a significant segment of the blue-collar population—in this instance, the construction workers—is breaking its 35-year attachment to the other major party. The general tone of the "hard hat" demonstrations and statements of participants in the violence that accompanied one of the demonstrations suggests strongly that many blue-collar workers view themselves as part of Nixon's "silent majority," driven at last to speak out against the disrupters, the radicals, the disloyal in American society. And the gist of their message was an embrace of the Nixon presidency.

About the time the hard hats began their series of demonstrations in New York in early May, government specialists were completing a study of the blue-collar worker which the President had commissioned in the summer of 1969. A confidential memorandum on the report, leaked to the press in late June,[1] revealed the administration's interest in the blue-collar worker's economic and social problems. To many commentators the memorandum also suggested the administration's interest in his political potential. "People in the blue-collar class," the memorandum stated, "feel like forgotten people—those for whom the government and society have limited, if any, direct concern." They were, therefore, "over-ripe for a political response to the pressing needs they feel so keenly."

What is interesting about this development is not that a new "forgotten man" has come forward, but that a fully recognized figure in the American picture is being perceived somewhat

---

[1] First accounts of the contents of the memorandum appeared in the June 30, 1970, issues of *The New York Times* and *The Wall Street Journal*, which described the report as "confidential" to the President. A government-reproduced copy of the memorandum became generally available without fanfare on Aug. 4.

differently than in the past. Actually the blue-collar worker has long been visible—politically, socially, economically. Many would say he has not been particularly silent and he has been quite successful in making known his demands and winning responses to them, at the collective bargaining table at least. What is new is seeing the blue-collar worker not simply in terms of a unionist seeking higher wages and job benefits, but in his broader human dimensions as a man whose private life is being buffeted by the disrupting currents of his time.

Interest centers particularly on the working man as an exemplar of outraged middle America, economically pressed despite high wages and numerous income-protecting programs, angry over social disorder (crime, riots, campus unrest, anti-war protests), resentful of paying taxes to support programs for nonworkers (college students and welfare recipients), suspicious of minority encroachment on his job, fearful of deterioration of his neighborhood, and imbued with a surging patriotic fervor that strikes some observers as being tinged with jingoism.

Administration Report on Blue-Collar Workers

Special significance has been attached to the administration memorandum[2] because it is the product of a study by an interdepartmental panel headed by George P. Shultz as Secretary of Labor. Shortly after the final draft was written— by Jerome M. Rosow, Assistant Secretary of Labor for Policy Evaluation and Research—Shultz moved up to a new position as Director of the Office of Management and Budget. From this lofty post in the White House Shultz has broad leverage for pressing all departments of government to take positive action on any recommendations of the panel that meet the President's approval.

The Rosow memorandum is concerned with those workers in blue-collar employment who earn between $5,000 and $10,000 a year. Together with members of their families—and most of these workers are family men—they comprise some 70 million Americans or two-fifths of all American families. Not all workers in this earnings range are in blue-collar employment, but the blue-collar group tends to be more fixed at this level of earnings than the better-educated white-collar worker. At some levels of white-collar employment, however, the economic problems and the general outlook are quite similar to those of the blue-collar group.

---

[2] *The Problem of the Blue-Collar Worker,* subtitled "A Memorandum for the Secretary [of Labor]." It was delivered to President Nixon in June 1970.

Much has been made of the rising affluence of the American worker, and certainly his pay is high by the standards of the past. But the Rosow memorandum finds the blue-collar man is in an "economic squeeze." The wage is not bad if he is single or even newly married, especially if his wife takes a job, but when the children arrive and begin to grow up his expenses mount more rapidly than his income.

It is precisely when his children reach their teens and family budget costs are at their peak that two things happen to the bulk of such male breadwinners:

They reach a plateau in their capacity to earn by promotion or advancement; their expenses continue to rise, as the last family members are born, as they become home owners, as car and home equipment pressures mount, as the children may become ready for college, or support is needed for aging parents.

Inflation had intensified the problem. Wages had advanced 20 per cent since 1965, but real earnings in terms of purchasing power had hardly changed. "These men are on a treadmill, chasing the illusion of higher standards....Their only hope seems to be continued pressure for higher wages." The only way they can maintain their standard of living is to dip into savings, have wives go out to work,[3] moonlight on a second, part-time job, or keep up the pressure for higher wages.

Not all of the blue-collar man's troubles were economic, though most of them bore on his economic situation. He was sensitive about the "low status" of his work. "According to union leaders, the blue-collar worker increasingly feels that his work has no 'status' in the eyes of society, the media, or even his own children." Other problems said to "bug" him were: fear of violent crime, now spilling over from the inner city to the outer rings of the metropolis where many blue-collar workers live; "minority inroads in housing, schools, and jobs"; and growth of social programs for which he is taxed but from which he is excluded, though his wages are "only a notch or so above the liberal states' welfare payments." It all added up to that feeling of being left out in the cold. The report recommended the following steps to help meet blue-collar grievances:

Upgrade blue-collar jobs by counseling, in-plant instruction, job-skill courses in community colleges, etc.

Provide part-time work and child-care facilities for blue-collar wives.

---

[3] But "high transportation costs, wage discrimination, and lack of education and training...discourage many...wives...or minimize their contribution to family income."

More support for community colleges, attended by blue-collar youth, and provisions for workers to finish high school or take two-year college courses at night.

Tax relief, possibly raising tax exemption for older children and raising deduction for cost of child care while mother works.

Public relations effort to raise status of work: national craftsman awards, stamp issues, films, etc.

More mass transit, low-cost recreation facilities, mortgage money to lower housing costs.

Improve on-job accident insurance.

The report suggested that the federal government become a model blue-collar employer "by careful attention to such things as upgrading possibilities, subsidized child care, part-time employment for women, and partially subsidized recreation and vacation facilities for low-income federal workers."

Construction Workers' Attack on Peace Parade

The existence of the memorandum attracted particular interest because its contents were disclosed on the heels of a series of pro-Nixon demonstrations, one of them entailing violence, by construction workers in the downtown financial district of New York. It was this development that gave a new social and political meaning to the label "hard hats." Though construction workers in New York are enjoying a boom that has pushed earnings of some of the highest-skilled, overtime-working men to as much as $18,000 a year, these workers share many of the grievances outlined in the Rosow report and they are in an industry subject to fluctuations in employment.

"Hard hat" demonstrations were significant as an outburst of blue-collar sentiment directed to issues other than economic and as a sign of blue-collar willingness to take to the streets in the manner of other protest groups. They constituted a counter-attack against other protesters—students, radicals, and anti-Viet Nam War activists. The "hard hats," working on construction sites from where they could view the street theater of the protesters and being known for their toughness and physical prowess, became a natural vanguard of counter-protest.

Worker impatience first boiled over during lunch hour on May 6. A number of construction men threw beer cans and clumps of asphalt at students demonstrating in the street for peace in Viet Nam. Two days later, again at lunch hour, several hundred workers, wearing their work helmets and carrying American flags, left the construction sites to march in the streets. The march became a rampage. The workers stormed City Hall to force the raising of the American flag which had been lowered to half-mast, on orders of Mayor John V. Lindsay, in mourning for the students who had been killed by National Guard fire at Kent State University. Some workers broke into Pace College on the route of their march to attack students who had made the peace sign. Others chased and beat anyone at hand who seemed, by dress, age or manner, to be unsympathetic to the marchers. Eyewitnesses said the workers had used their helmets, their fists, and their hand tools in the attacks. Some 70 persons were injured.

According to news accounts, New York City police, who had been detailed to the area in expectation of the demonstration,[4] made little effort to stop the violence. When word of the event reached Mayor Lindsay, he went on television. Obviously angry, he denounced the violence which he called "tough and organized" and criticized the police for making little effort to protect the public from "wanton violence." Police officials retorted that their men on the scene were outnumbered by demonstrators.

The May 8 demonstration "was the wild start of two weeks of almost daily noon-hour, flag-waving, bellicose, damn-Lindsay...and praise-Nixon countermarches through downtown New York,"[5] though there was little further violence. On some occasions the construction workers were joined by longshoremen and others, including a few white-collar sympathizers. The series reached a climax on May 20 when more than 100,000 blue-collar workers, mainly skilled workmen in the building trades, marched between the skyscrapers in downtown New York, carrying flags and singing patriotic songs. Like the previous demonstrations, the general tone of the march, indicated by banners and shouted slogans, was anti-Lindsay and pro-Nixon.

The political significance of the march was underlined six days later, May 26, when President Nixon received 23 leaders of New York buildings trades' and longshoremen's unions and met with them at the White House for 45 minutes. They presented the President with a hard hat and told him that it "would stand as a symbol, along with our great flag, for

---

[4] Spokesmen for the workers said the march was spontaneous. However, the city government had received advance warnings that it was to take place. Some accounts cited evidence that employers of the men had encouraged them and that right-wing groups helped organize the demonstration.

[5] Richard Rogin, "Joe Kelly Has Reached His Boiling Point," *New York Times Magazine*, June 28, 1970, p. 14.

freedom and patriotism to our beloved country." The President accepted the hat and thanked the men for their support which he found reassuring and "very meaningful." No mention was made of the violence.[6]

Hard Hat as Anti-Liberal, Pro-Nixon Symbol

Since then the hard hat with a flag pasted on its surface has become the symbol of a conglomeration of attitudes adding up to an anti-liberal, right-wing position strongly in support of Nixon and Vice President Spiro T. Agnew personally, aggressively patriotic, hostile to manifestations of the youth culture, and openly anti-intellectual. Depending on the observer, the hard hat movement may represent a welcome show of stability, decency and love-of-country against the forces of anarchism and moral degeneracy in the nation, or it may represent a frightening show of a fascist potential in middle America.

Hard hat demonstrations sparked a boom in the sale and display of flags of all sizes. Flags began to pop up everywhere: on auto and truck windshields, on hats, lapels, construction sites. A firm named Patriotic Enterprises, Ltd., advertised in *The Wall Street Journal*, July 21: "Own a Real Hard Hat" with a molded flag decal on its side that glows in the dark; price $5. Almost overnight the displaying of a flag began to mean advocacy of the hard-hat position.

Many efforts were made to plumb the meaning and depth of this new manifestation of polarization in American society. "While the violence of the construction workers is of course indefensible," commented the right-wing weekly *Human Events*, May 23, 1970, "there can be no doubt that it reflects a national mood of anger and resistance to the techniques of confrontation practiced by the New Left and anti-war militants." Writing in the left-of-center *Nation* a few weeks later (June 15), Fred J. Cook said: "Fascism is a word to be used with discretion...but it is undeniable that its elements could be felt [in the hard hat demonstration]."

Jimmy Breslin, from still another vantage point, observed that, knowing the antipathies and the toughness of the workers, he was not surprised at the violence. "The strange thing

---

[6] *The Wall Street Journal* was among critics of the administration's failure to condemn the violence of the earlier demonstration. "Now that the President has donned a hard hat," the *Journal* stated in an editorial May 28, "we would forgive any construction worker who believed Mr. Nixon's embrace included not only those who attended the rally but those who bashed heads as well."

about it is that it took so long to happen." A lot of the fault lay with the "arrogance [of those in the anti-war movement] toward people who work with their hands."[7] Alvin Toffler, author of *Future Shock* (1970), suggested that the "hard hats" were suffering from a widespread psychic distress arising out of modern man's effort to absorb the increasingly rapid changes in his immediate environment.

"The impact of sudden change leaves the person anxious, bewildered," Toffler wrote. For the "hard hat" as for his opposite number, the kid cop-out, "the gut issue is not so much race [or] war...but the rate at which novelty explodes into their lives, smashing their lifelong routines and values."[8] Construction workers interviewed by reporters had simpler answers. One said: "We built this city with our hands. We put our sweat and blood into [it]....Now these punks want to bring it all down with bombs and riots. They ain't American. Send 'em to Russia."

Blue-Collar Work in Changing America

THE NEW INTEREST in the blue-collar worker raises questions about the way a man's occupation affects his outlook on life, his values, his life style—and his political orientation. Most men relate to society chiefly in terms of the work they do, hence the value society places on their work has much to do with their attitudes toward that society. In a stable, hierarchal society the low-status worker may be resigned to his position, but in a restless, socially mobile society low-caste workers are likely to chafe against the evaluation placed on their work or to seek work of higher status.

Class distinctions by occupation prevail in all societies. "Any industrial society will have to evolve a prestige system closely tied to occupation, for an industrial system takes so much energy and attention and has such control over subordinate aspects of life that it pushes work activity to the forefront of thought and value."[9] Generally speaking, the physical worker is accorded a lower status than the one who works with his mind. But the line drawn between blue- and

---

[7] Jimmy Breslin, "One Way to End the War," *New York*, June 22, 1970, p. 26.

[8] Alvin Toffler, "New York Faces Future Shock," *New York*, July 27, p. 20.

[9] Joseph A. Kahl, *The American Class Structure* (1957), p. 62.

white-collar employment in the United States does not make so sharp a division by class; "blue-collar worker" today lacks the connotations of the older term "working class," which used to distinguish between ordinary wage-earners and persons in the professions and in business. Differences in skills and earnings within each collar-color group have blurred class distinctions between the two.

The terms blue-collar and white-collar originated as a casual way of distinguishing wage-earners whose work was primarily manual or involved tools and machines from those whose work was primarily mental, requiring the use of literate skills or involving the relationship between people. The terms appeared in government tabulations of labor statistics about a decade ago;[10] certain occupational categories were listed under one or the other collar-color heading. Blue-collar listings today include craftsmen (skilled workers), foremen (in shops, factories, and on construction jobs), operatives and kindred workers (typically semi-skilled operators of machines in manufacturing) and nonfarm laborers (unskilled workers). The white-collar components are professional and technical, managers, officials and nonfarm proprietors, clerical workers and sales workers. Other major occupational divisions outside the collar designations are service workers and farm workers.

	Blue-collar workers	% of total labor force	White-collar workers	% of total labor force
1900	10,400,000	36	5,100,000	18
1920	12,100,000	29	10,529,000	25
1940	16,300,000	36	14,630,000	33
1950	23,336,000	39	22,373,000	37
1960	24,211,000	36	28,726,000	43
1970*	27,663,000	38	37,981,000	48

Within the blue-collar group, the gap between the unskilled and the skilled is wide in terms of earning capacity and prestige. This is nothing new. Even in ancient times, the gifted artisan was more highly prized than the ditch-digger. In the American colonies and during the early years of nationhood, skilled workers enjoyed considerable respect and commanded high wages because the need for their services was so great. Bricklayers, cabinetmakers, carpenters, coopers, glaziers, glovers, hatters, masons, printers, sadlers, sailmakers, saw-

---

[10] Since then the government has retroactively applied the same collar-color standards to labor statistics gathered in prior decades. See table above.

yers, shipwrights, smiths, shoemakers, tailors, tanners, weavers—all prospered and many lived well by contemporary standards. In sharp contrast, the common laborer worked for a pittance and his standard of living was not much better than that of the peasant in Europe.

Effects of Industrial Revolution on Worker Role

"A constant scarcity of workers served to maintain wage rates well above European levels in the 17th and 18th centuries; the opportunities for advancement in the New World nullified the hard and fast class lines that were the feudal heritage of the Old World, and the frontier generally fostered a spirit of sturdy individualism."[11] Legislation adopted by the Massachusetts Bay Colony in the 17th century to place a ceiling on wages and forbid prospering workmen to wear dressy clothes proved a futile effort to maintain the occupational class lines of the Old World. The demand for labor made the laws unenforceable.

Since he operated in a socially mobile society, the gifted workman could rise readily above his early station in life. Many who came to the New World as indentured servants took up an independent trade after working out their terms of service, then opened up shops and hired helpers for wages. As the cities grew, the shops expanded and more workers were hired, though the master usually continued to work side by side with his employees. The Industrial Revolution disrupted this work pattern and transformed the artisan who produced a complete product—a shoe, a set of harness, a sail—into an adjunct of a mass production process. A labor historian has described the psychological impact on the worker:

> Industrialization and the concentration of power posed an elemental threat to blue-collar workers. Their conception of self— like that of so many other Americans—was rooted in the conviction that each individual enjoyed freedom and independence, with the power to shape his own destiny. A commitment to independence and individualism—touchstones of the American experience —bound the worker to his society. Yet the very experiences that had long given meaning to these values seemed to have ended by 1900. Consolidation and mass production threatened to subsume the individual in an impersonal industrial complex in which he was but an expendable part.[12]

It is not surprising that the drive for shorter hours—a movement "invested with more emotional energy and pressed with

---

[11] Foster Rhea Dulles, *Labor in America* (third edition, 1966), pp. 1-2.

[12] Jerold S. Auerbach, introduction to *American Labor: The Twentieth Century* (Auerbach, ed., 1969), p. xxv.

greater vigor than any other demand of working people in the 19th century"—followed the growth of the factory system. "Formerly work had been leisurely and spasmodic, carried out in the midst of the family and interwoven with other aspects of life. Then it was segregated, militarized, highly disciplined, and abstracted from the natural rhythm and spontaneity of human activity."[13] Oppressive working conditions, the remoteness of the owner from the work place, and the resistance of expanding industry to unionization efforts widened the chasm between the worker and those who seemed to be in control of his fate.

In their two books on "Middletown," the Lynds traced the transformation of the occupational caste system in a typical midwestern market town under the impact of industrialization. The town traders and craftsmen in 1890 had shared the traditions of their rural past; income and prestige derived from the individual's personal effort as he moved up the ladder from unskilled to skilled and possibly to boss (but still a craftsman) status. Thirty-four years later the Lynds found two major classes in the town—the business class and the working class. The cleavage between them was absolute. "The mere fact of being born upon one or the other side of the watershed roughly formed by these two groups is the most significant single cultural factor tending to influence what one does all day long throughout one's life," they wrote.[14] Returning to "Middletown" in the mid-1930s, the Lynds found that a further stage of industrialization had created gradations of status within the working class. There was now a hierarchy of labor in descending order from "trusted foremen, building trades craftsmen...highly skilled machinists" to semi-skilled and unskilled workers, chiefly factory machine operatives, truckmen, and laborers—"the mass of wage earners."[15]

Alienation Despite Gains in Wages and Prestige

Blue-collar work gained considerable prestige from the mid-1930s onward. The rise of unionization, and then the years of rising wages, brought the manual worker to a par or better than many white-collar workers and helped to erase lower-caste implications of the term "working class."

Collective bargaining...has erased collar-color as a qualifying factor in access to pensions, vacations, company-financed insur-

---

[13] Arthur M. Ross, "Work and Leisure in the Round of Life," *Labor in a Changing America* (1966), p. 187.

[14] Robert S. and Helen M. Lynd, *Middletown* (1929), p. 24. Middletown was their code name for Muncie, Ind., where their sociological study was conducted.

[15] Robert S. and Helen M. Lynd, *Middletown in Transition* (1937), p. 460.

AVERAGE WEEKLY EARNINGS,* JUNE 1970

Mining $162.78	Wholesale Trade $137.42
Contract construction 197.12	
Manufacturing (production	Retail Trade 83.11
workers) 134.40	
Highest average: Petroleum	Finance, Insurance Real
and coal products 182.75	Estate 111.50
Lowest average: Apparel and	
other textile products 84.01	Services 96.95

*Non-supervisory workers only.

ance programs, and other perquisites once reserved for executives and office employees. And the trend toward leveling the divide between blue-collar and white-collar treatment has made its way into pay envelopes through supplemental unemployment benefits and related earnings plans.

These now assure workers in automobile, can, steel and many other basic industries of 86 per cent to 95 per cent of their normal weekly take-home pay for a full year after layoff....On the Atlantic and Gulf docks...regular longshoremen have a guarantee of at least 2,000 hours pay a year....International Business Machines Corporation...decided as long ago as 1958 to abolish hourly wages for its factory employees and give them weekly salaries just like everyone else.[16]

Despite these gains, a feeling of alienation, of being outside the realm of power and of being looked down upon, has persisted in the blue-collar ranks. The Rosow memorandum expressed the belief that this feeling had deepened in the last few years. Industry's growing reliance on professional and technical personnel contributed to the skilled worker's sense of having been downgraded . The memorandum stated:

The American working man has lost relative class status with the growth of higher education....The blue-collar worker increasingly feels that his work has no 'status' in the eyes of society, the media, or even his own children. While the nation has, in recent years, sold the importance of science and technology to our younger people, it has neglected to communicate the importance of some 10 million skilled blue-collar workers who are responsible for transforming the ideas of scientists and the plans of engineers into tangible goods and services....Schools tend to reinforce this tendency, since most teachers know little about blue-collar work. So do the media....

"The 'myth of the happy worker'...is still just that," the author of *Technological Man* wrote. The "alienation from work" was particularly noted at the semi-skilled level. "A

---

[16] A. H. Raskin, "The Labor Movement Must Start Moving," *Harvard Business Review*, January-February 1970, p. 116.

basic fact about semi-skilled working class life: it is on a flat level. There are few differences in pay or responsibility from job to job, from year to year. There is not too much point in working hard to get somewhere for there is no place to go."[17] An article in *Fortune* described "the deep dislike of the job and the desire to escape" of production workers in automobile plants. This was shown in high rates of absenteeism, tardiness, turnover, and discipline problems. Dull jobs, once manned by "unschooled immigrant labor and farm youths," are less tolerated by young blue-collar workers of today. "In their present temper," the author wrote, they "would probably like nothing better than to down tools for a rousing great strike."[18]

Sensitivity of Ethnic Worker to Social Pressures

A key fact about blue-collar workers is that many of them are "ethnics"—one or two generations removed from the immigrants. Though the influence of the foreign culture—and the experience in the American ghetto—fades in time, certain sensitivities remain. The immigrant arrived penniless and willingly took the least desirable jobs at the lowest pay. He knew that the larger community looked down on him, especially if he came from eastern or southern Europe. In the steel mills at the turn of the century "an unbridgeable gulf separated...the 'hunky' and the English-speaking workmen....The strange-tongued Slavic peasant repelled the native workers." Only the "hunky" was considered fit for work on the blast furnaces.[19]

Today's descendants of those immigrants may have a standard of living beyond the dreams of their immigrant forbears, but they have a keen sense of the years of drudgery and hardship that preceded their rise. They therefore react negatively to what the Rosow report describes as "the pressure of constant succession by lower status groups, especially minorities." This is particularly true of those who live in mixed neighborhoods or in neighborhoods adjoining those of the less affluent. "As the minorities move up a bit, they squeeze these [blue-collar] people," the memorandum stated. "Minority inroads in housing, schools, and jobs create fears."

---

[17] Victor C. Ferkiss, *Technological Man* (1969), pp. 206, 210.

[18] Judson Gooding, "Blue-Collar Blues on the Assembly Line," *Fortune*, July 1970, p. 71. Renewal of three-year contracts in the automobile industry, due to expire in September 1970, are now under negotiation.

[19] David Brody, *Steelworkers in America: The Nonunion Era* (Harvard Historical Monographs XLV, 1960)

The grievances of ethnic Americans in the blue-collar group were forcefully expressed at a conference held in Washington, June 15-19, 1970, by the Task Force on Urban Problems of the United States Catholic Conference. The meetings drew together priests, politicians and community workers from the inner cities of major industrial centers in an effort to develop a program for overcoming the bad feeling between white ethnics and blacks. The Catholic Church has a special interest in this problem because many of the 40 million people of European descent in the older industrial cities are of the Catholic faith. "I realized that a lot of people were resisting the black revolution," said Monsignor Geno C. Baroni, program director for the task force, "and that the largest group was the white ethnics in the large industrial cities."

Barbara Mikulski, director of the Southeast Community Organization in Baltimore, drew considerable attention at the conference when she said:

> America is not a melting pot. It is a sizzling cauldron for the ethnic American who feels that he has been politically courted and legally extorted by both government and private enterprise.
>
> The ethnic American is sick of being stereotyped as a racist and dullard by phony white liberals, pseudo-black militants and patronizing bureaucrats. He pays the bill for every major government program and gets nothing or little in the way of return.
>
> Tricked by the political rhetoric of illusionary funding for black-oriented social programs, he turns his anger to race—when he himself is the victim of class prejudice. He has worked hard all his life to become a 'good American';...then he is made fun of because he likes the flag.

Running counter to a popular belief that the ethnic is racist, the Louis Harris polling organization reported that a survey it conducted in March 1970 indicated that "white native Americans" were more likely to be hostile to blacks than "white ethnics" were.[20] The poll had been commissioned by the National Urban League and its findings were announced in New York on Aug. 19, 1970, by Whitney Young, the league director, who. acknowledged that he was "somewhat surprised." Young noted a correlation between high income and liberality of racial views. But Young suggested that the correlation between blue-collar income and racial intolerance was modified, at least among the ethnic groups surveyed, by their ability to identify with lower-class minority workers.

---

[20] "White Native Americans" were defined as persons having at least one grandparent who was Protestant and whose country of origin was Germany, England, Ireland, Scotland or the Scandinavian countries; "white ethnics" were identified as persons whose grandparents were not Protestant and who were of Polish, Irish Catholic or Italian origin.

Blue-Collar Man and Politics of 1970s

WHATEVER HIS GRIEVANCES, the blue-collar man in 1970 can hardly complain of neglect by the political planners. In his new volatile mood, with no one quite sure which way or how far he will go, he seems due for an ardent political court-ship by both major parties, potential third parties, and special-interest factions seeking to build constituencies within the parties. A key question is whether the blue-collar man will remain in the Democratic coalition that Franklin D. Roosevelt put together 35 years ago.[21] Blue-collar loyalty to the Demo-crats arose from the New Deal, which not only supported the industrial unions' struggle for recognition and the prin-ciple of collective bargaining but enacted social legislation that was of benefit primarily to the blue-collar worker—work relief, minimum wage, 40-hour week, unemployment com-pensation and so forth.

The rising affluence of the blue-collar worker in the years that followed World War II led to considerable speculation about his political loyalties. Fortunately for the Democrats, the wage gains and home ownership in the suburbs did not convert the downtrodden worker of the New Deal past into a solid-citizen Republican. Samuel Lubell wrote in 1951, report-ing on the first of the series of voter-sentiment surveys he has made over the years, "The rising prosperity of the last years ...has subtly transformed the internal makeup of the Demo-cratic coalition, lifting many of its members to a 'have' status ....But in the main the poor and underprivileged have remained loyal to the Democratic party. The new middle class, which has developed over the last two decades, seems as Demo-cratic by custom as the older middle class elements are instinctively Republican."[22]

The coalition held, with some weakening, during the 1950s and 1960s. It even withstood the Republican choice of a national hero for President in 1952 and 1956. The overwhelm-

---

[21] It is of interest to recall that it was during, not before, the first Roosevelt adminis-tration that the labor component entered the Democratic coalition. Roosevelt was so little concerned about labor during the 1932 campaign that he "had not even bothered to make a major labor speech" but by 1936 a powerful new element had become part of the coalition: "organized labor, endowed...with a new stake in the federal govern-ment and...determined to keep a friendly administration in Washington."—Arthur M. Schlesinger Jr., *The Politics of Upheaval* (1960), pp. 592-593.

[22] Samuel Lubell, *The Future of American Politics* (1951), pp. 58-59.

ing popularity of President Eisenhower cut into the blue-collar vote but, still, 85 per cent of the Democrats in 1956 held fast with their party's candidate, Adlai E. Stevenson. The Democratic party, with the strong assistance of organized labor, overcame the lure of third-party candidate George C. Wallace in 1968 and retained its hold on the blue-collar worker. "Democrats on the national level are viewed...as the party of the workingman, the intellectual, the Jews, the blacks, many ethnic Catholics, and, until recently, southerners," wrote Richard Scammon and Ben Wattenberg, authors of a 1970 survey of the political scene. "Americans don't readily change their basic overview of politics," they added. Hubert H. Humphrey, the Democratic presidential nominee in 1968, "raised the old banner of the Democratic party and most of the people who had saluted it in the past found they could not easily abandon it or the political overview that it had for so long represented"—"And back they came: the Jews; the blacks, the poor; the big-city ethnic Catholics; the union men who had toyed with supporting Wallace; the intellectuals who had been for Eugene McCarthy."[23]

Evidence of Loosening of Democratic Allegiance

Nevertheless most political observers, including Scammon and Wattenberg, sense that the scene is shifting under the pressures of social change. The blue-collar voter stayed with the Democratic party because he thought of it as the party of the working man, as he thought of the Republican as the party of big business. But that seems to be changing. Scammon and Wattenberg wrote that for the 1970s "the battlefield shows signs of splitting into two battlefields: the old economic one and the new social one that deals with crime, drugs, racial pressure, and disruption."

Reporting in 1970 on his latest round of questioning voters, Lubell noted that "a strange new politics of impatience" had transformed the tempo and character of American politics. Worker prosperity had made a political impact at last, but in an indirect and unexpected way. "The unprecedented boom of recent years...quickened racial frictions...and is eroding the effective power of all government, aggravating political conflict generally. In the process loyalty to all political parties has been loosened, which in turn is changing voter psychology." The economic cleavage between Republicans and Democrats held in 1968 but it "no longer structures enough of the vote to

---

[23] Richard M. Scammon and Ben J. Wattenberg, *The Real Majority* (1970), p. 172.

give either party a majority." He predicted that "with each election to come, the hold of New Deal memories will loosen, while the weight of the free-floating voters is likely to be felt more strongly."[24]

The American worker, true to his historic role in politics, shows no inclination to form a labor party. He thus remains available for courtship by all political parties. They try to gauge his mood and inclination, particularly if the major parties are in a close race. Politicians now sense that the working man—as distinct from the labor leader—is being churned about and may possibly be dislodged from his customary political alignment.

Coolness of U.S. Workers to Radical Appeals

Over the years the American working man has been both a rebel and a conservative, but on the whole he has leaned to the conservative side. He fought for economic benefits at a time when such benefits were contrary to established policy. But in relatively good times, with unemployment down and wages rising, he supported the status quo. The latter position seems to reflect his general orientation toward the sober virtues of the traditional family man.

Workingmen's parties sprang up in a number of American towns in the late 1820s under the stress of a depression and the indifference of Federalists and Whigs, but the labor-party movement faded when its objectives were taken over by the Jacksonians. "Only when the major parties proved unresponsive to labor's demands did the [early] union movement turn to independent action. For the same general reasons, labor's independent political efforts ordinarily subsided quickly— either owing to improvement in economic climate or because a major party embraced its cause."[25]

Severe depressions have raised the threat of a revolutionary movement among unemployed workers in times past. But despite the infusion of Socialist thinking during the formative years of the labor movement, the threat never materialized. Coxey's Army, a band of unemployed workmen who marched on Washington in 1894, riled many conservative figures "who viewed with alarm any tendency of the lower strata of society

---

[24] Samuel Lubell, *The Hidden Crisis in American Politics* (1970), pp. 17, 22, 242.
[25] Charles M. Rehmus, "Labor in American Politics," *Labor in a Changing America*, William Haber, ed., 1966, p. 255.

to assert themselves."[26] But Coxeyism was essentially reformist and was more allied with Populism than with revolution. The failure of left-wing radicalism to win mass support from the American blue-collar worker, despite Communist infiltration of some unions during the 1930s, testifies to the basic conservatism of the working class.

> The very correspondence of workers' values with the values of a society committed to industrial capitalism has long been a source of unease both to intellectuals and to radicals. Since Marx wrote the Communist Manifesto, generations of critics hostile to capitalism have waited for the workers of the world—or at least those of the United States—to unite and revolt. Yet workers in this country seem to have felt that they had far more to lose than their chains. Consequently radicals and intellectuals who channeled their passion toward the downtrodden worker...have suffered from unrequited love.[27]

Efforts of the Students for a Democratic Society to link their cause with labor's have been dismal failures. SDS offers to support labor strikes have been rudely rebuffed. Union leaders in New York were reported in *Encounter* magazine to have postponed a strike vote against Columbia University in April 1968 so that their pickets would not seem to be giving legitimacy to the students' revolt. Workers' hostility to student radicals is not peculiar to the United States. Students tried and failed just as abysmally to win a revolutionary brotherhood with workers in England, France, Germany, Italy and Japan.

"The working class in democratic, pluralist societies has refused to rise to the revolutionary bait....This immunity to revolutionary slogans among workers and trade unionists is demonstrable by a simple fact: revolutionary socialism or communism has yet to be established in an industrial country through an electoral victory....The industrial worker has as always grasped with a fine sociological instinct that the revolutionary program actually means that the average man will not have it better but *worse*."[28]

The more moderate leadership of the peace movement is beginning to grasp the same lesson—that the great American middle, with its large component of blue-collar workers and their families, is not easily drawn to any cause that looks revolutionary or offends its conservative sense of values. Sam

---

[26] Donald L. McMurry, *Coxey's Army: A Study of the Industrial Army Movement of 1894* (originally published 1929; 1968 edition), p. 268.

[27] Jerold S. Auerbach, *op. cit.*, p. xxix.

[28] Arnold Beichman, "Beware of the Proctors!" *Encounter*, August 1970, pp. 53-54, 56-57.

Brown, who led the youth-for-Eugene McCarthy campaign in 1968, has now taken the peace movement to task for failing to reach "the right wing of potential peace supporters." He advocates that the peace movement detach itself from factions that combine opposition to Viet Nam policy with a call for revolution. He argues that the peace movement must recognize middle America's distaste for long hair, campus uprisings, confrontations with police, revolutionary rhetoric, obscene speech, and flaunting of sexual freedom. "The potential peace voters respond favorably to the calm, authoritative demeanor of the President," Brown wrote. "They may dislike the war, but they dislike radicals far more."[29]

Whether the worker is resistant to the siren call of the extreme right may depend on how much he fears or detests the left. George C. Wallace pitched much of his appeal to the anti-intellectual prejudices of the blue-collar class. While he succeeded in cracking the Democratic coalition in the South in 1968, he made only minor gains among blue-collar workers elsewhere. The impression that Wallace was "anti-labor" did much to keep blue-collar Democrats in line, even those who responded favorably to his attacks on "pseudo-intellectual government, where an elect, elite group have written guidelines in bureaus and court decisions...looking down their noses at the average man on the street, the glassworker, the steelworker, the autoworker...saying to him that you do not know how to get up in the morning...unless we write you a guideline."[30]

If the working man is truly resistant to extremes of both right and left, the contest for his vote between the major parties will depend on (1) whether Republicans can allay working-class fears that a GOP victory will undermine labor gains[31] and (2) whether the economic issue will take second place to the issue of social unrest. The way the wind blows now, it looks as if the "law and order" theme may be the dominant one in the blue-collar precincts.

---

[29] Sam Brown, "The Politics of Peace," *The Washington Monthly*, August 1970, p. 26.

[30] Quoted by Scammon and Wattenberg, *op. cit.*, p. 62.

[31] "Fears that a Republican administration would undermine Social Security, Medicare, collective bargaining and aid to education played a major part in keeping socially conservative blue-collar workers...loyal to the 1968 Democratic candidate. Assuming that a Nixon administration can dispel these apprehensions, it ought to be able to repeat—with much more permanence—Eisenhower's great blue-collar success of 1956."—Kevin P. Phillips, *The Emerging Republican Majority* (1969), p. 464.

CHANGING CORPORATE WORLD

by

William Gerber

SOCIETY'S CHALLENGE TO CORPORATIONS
Demands on Companies to Show Social Concern
Unrest in Middle Management; New Yearnings
Campus Dissatisfaction With Values of Business
Erosion of 'Organization Man' Outlook in Sixties

EVOLUTION OF U.S. BUSINESS ATTITUDES
Robber-Baron Mentality of Late 19th Century
Stirrings of Corporate Soul in Muckraking Era
Rise of New Class of Professional Executives
Impact of White-Collar Crime on Business Image

COMING DECISIONS FOR EXECUTIVE SUITES
Training of Executives to Challenge Tradition
Issue of Accountability: Stockholders or Public
Role of Executives in Promoting Social Reform
Area of Agreement Between Youth and Business

1 9 7 1
Feb. 3

CHANGING CORPORATE WORLD

A MERICAN CORPORATIONS seemed an unlikely place only a short time ago for the phrase "social responsibility" to fall from every lip. Yet hardly any business executive neglects the phrase in his speeches these days. It is true that there may be no precise understanding among the listeners as to how the words would be applied. But the very fact that they are spoken at all says much about the state of the corporate world. Business leaders are changing, whether grudgingly or willingly, to meet some of the changing attitudes of society.

Business literature is replete with self-analysis and wonderment in the midst of attack from many sides. Corporation executives seem no less puzzled than many other Americans as to why young people entering the labor force—even in a time of job scarcity—are less enchanted with the so-called Protestant ethic of hard work and upward striving than their parents and grandparents. Consumerism is another current of opinion the business community must reckon with. By no means confined to the young, it is questioning and perhaps tarnishing some cherished notions about mass production, advertising and planned obsolescence. Not only that, company management now is beginning to recognize a need to answer the public, not just some legal authority, for industrial pollution or discriminatory hiring.

A corporation can sometimes be goaded into taking remedial action, whether from a bad conscience or from fear of bad publicity. The latter may entail such attendant problems as a product boycott or, in extreme cases, a factory or office bombing. But if "business as usual" is no longer the order of the day, it can also be said that "corporation democracy" has not yet arrived, at least not fully enough to satisfy those who advocate it as a way of making big business responsive to the demands of society at large. To management, extreme responsiveness may mean shrunken profits, or none at all.

Where should its allegiance lie, with the stockholder or the citizen?

Dr. Milton Friedman, the University of Chicago professor whom *Fortune* magazine describes (December 1970) as "the leading fundamentalist of classical economic thought today," sees the answer clearly. Those executives who talk about social responsibilities, Friedman contends, are usurping their function. They are enjoined, first and foremost, to make money for the stockholders. While he acknowledges that businessmen must abide by law and ethical custom, he sees little room for social concerns in the board rooms.

One of the most publicized attempts to force corporate change has been the Campaign to Make General Motors Responsible—"Campaign GM" for short—a project that has the support of consumer advocate Ralph Nader and the financial backing of the Stern foundation. When General Motors held its annual meeting in May 1970, two stockholders who held 12 shares proposed on behalf of Campaign GM that the company enlarge its board of directors to include three "representatives of the public" and establish a watchdog Committee for Corporate Responsibility. The Securities and Exchange Commission, which rules on proxy proposals, had disallowed other proposals, including one to require General Motors to improve automobile safety, cut pollution and take other actions in "the public interest." The proposals that were allowed were decisively defeated at the meeting but they apparently did not die there. "The battle last May could prove to be a mere skirmish compared to the one now developing in preparation for the 1971 annual meeting next May 21."[1]

John S. Fielden, dean of the Boston University College of Business Administration, believes that the discontent expressed on campus and in church during recent years is seeping into the business world and will invade the corporate hierarchy despite foot-dragging by inflexible managers. "Many managers I have talked with have wondered why university presidents and deans have not turned the hose on 'loud-mouth' demonstrators," he wrote. "They forget that these people [students] are our 'customers.' They forget that, in the early part of this

---

[1] Chris Welles, "The Greening of James Roche," *New York*, Dec. 21, 1970. The title links the name of the General Motors board chairman, James Roche, to Charles A. Reich's book *The Greening of America* (1970). The "greening," in Reich's view, is basically a repudiation of the "corporate state" through such manifestations as long hair, student protest, rock music, and rejection of careers by youth.

century, they too buckled under pressure when labor demanded a voice in management decisions...I think that for extremely complex reasons we are entering a period of increased corporate democracy with all that will be good and bad about it."[2]

Unrest in Middle Management; New Yearnings

Already, there is pressure from within big corporations for change. Signs of unrest are especially visible in the ranks of middle management. According to chroniclers of the scene, middle-level executives are becoming too impatient to spend 20 years or more with a single company awaiting step-by-step promotions to its upper echelons. Eugene Jennings, writing in *Psychology Today,* describes these executives as being representative of "mobicentric man," one who values motion and action "not because they lead to change but because they are change, and change is his ultimate value."[3] Nor is he the Organization Man, as portrayed by William H. Whyte in the 1950s, who placed company values ahead of private pleasure. Executives today, especially the younger ones, may willingly pass up promotions for the sake of staying where they like or of doing what they want.

Managers, lawyers, accountants, and others of the new breed were raised in affluence and schooled in tumult. As a consequence, they present not only a challenge to top leaders but an opportunity. The opportunity arises from the likelihood that the iconoclastic attitude of young executives is what aggressive corporations need for accelerated growth. Such corporations, tuned to the signal of consumerism and pressures for a pure environment, are faced with the need to do things that open-minded young people are best equipped to do—enlarge activities focused on social utility, acknowledge accountability to the public, and delegate large areas of responsibility to middle management whose prowess has been magnified by the computer. "Older men," according to management specialist Peter F. Drucker, "cannot do these jobs—not because they lack the necessary intelligence, but because they have the wrong conditioned reflexes."[4]

Curiously, bad economic conditions may have worsened rather than lessened the unrest of middle management. As

[2] John S. Fielden, *Harvard Business Review,* June 1970, pp. 15-16.

[3] Eugene Jennings, "Mobicentric Man," *Psychology Today,* July 1970, p. 35.

[4] Quoted in *Business Week,* Dec. 6, 1969, p. 146.

explained by George J. Berkwitt in *Dun's* magazine: "If the ideological gulf between those at the top and those in the middle has grown visibly wider in the past year or so, a major part of the blame...must be laid to the reeling economy.... With the corporate eye unblinkingly riveted on the bottom [profit] line, retrenchment—not risk-taking—has become the order of the day. So the innovative ideas that top management once listened to from bright middle managers in the big-budget days of the Soaring Sixties are being shunted aside in favor of tried-and-true techniques....And the upshot is that many a middle-echelon executive is bitterly resentful."[5]

Campus Dissatisfaction With Values of Business

To adjust to new talent, industry must every year hire college graduates, bring them into the organization, learn their strengths and interests, and make the best use of what they can offer. The first step in this process is recruitment. In the years from 1965 to 1969, recruitment became progressively difficult, because many young men with initiative, imagination, and ambition were shying away from business. Since then the shoe has been on the other foot. Defense cutbacks, the slowing of the economy, and the faster return of Viet Nam veterans to civilian life have combined to make the job outlook for the college graduating class of 1971 one of the worst in years.

The College Placement Council, a non-profit organization with headquarters at Bethlehem, Pa., surveyed more than 900 large employers early in the new year. The survey indicated that their job recruiters had scheduled 21 per cent fewer visits to college campuses than in 1970—itself a lean year—and that the companies were planning to hire 23 per cent fewer college graduares. However, the council said employment prospects for college seniors getting degrees in 1971 may not be as bleak as has been rumored. "There is reason for neither panic not blind optimism among students," the council commented. "Those with good qualifications and who actively seek jobs should find them. Those with marginal skills or those who just sit back waiting for a job may have problems."

U.S. News & World Report and *The Wall Street Journal* made similar surveys of the job scene. The magazine reported

---

[5] George J. Berkwitt, "Executives in Ferment," *Dun's*, January 1971, p. 23.

Dec. 21, 1970, that of 191 "well-known companies" it polled, only 60 thought that they would have more job openings for college graduates than in the previous year whereas 93 expected to have fewer such openings. The newspaper reported Jan. 20, 1971, that "college placement directors say they can't recall a time when so many companies were canceling scheduled visits."

Despite the turnabout in the job market, there was no persuasive evidence that the prevailing campus attitude toward business has been turned from negative to positive. In a poll conducted by *Fortune* among young adults and reported in its issue of June 1969, some 94 per cent of the students interviewed and 92 per cent of the non-students indicated they were convinced that business was too profit-minded and not concerned enough with public welfare.[6] The same student concerns have been expressed with regard to a number of professions, including law. Many law-school graduates are bypassing prestige firms to accept low-paying jobs in the legal-aid sections of poverty programs. To attract the young men and women they want, old-line law firms are often obliged to allow them time off to serve public causes.

New graduates are *against* several things in their employment, including emphasis on quantity instead of quality—a viewpoint to which President Nixon gave his blessing when he told Congress in the 1970 State of the Union message: "The time has come for...a quest not for a greater quantity of what we have, but for a new quality of life in America." New graduates, typically, profess to abhor aspects of technology that tend to reduce man to a machine-like function, and to find a distasteful amount of pretense and materialism in corporate life. They scorn time-honored maxims telling how to succeed in business.

They want instant responsibility, a chance for expression, opportunity to make an impact, and work which is visibly useful. The rejection of materialism expressed by the young stems from fear that "we have made Faust's bargain," that man "is swapping his soul for a summer cottage and a second car."[7] But for all their idealism, young executives

---

[6] A dissenting view was offered by Dr. James M. Lahiff, assistant professor of speech at the University of Georgia. He wrote in *Nation's Business,* May 1970: "Despite spotlighting of anti-business sentiment among campus groups and individuals, my own survey of more than 1,200 individual students in 28 colleges and universities across the country firmly supports the proposition that students, by and large, favor corporate business."

[7] Carl B. Kaufmann. *Man Incorporate: The Individual and His Work in an Organized Society* (1967), p. 11. See also "Alienated Youth," *E.R.R.*, 1966 Vol. II, p. 756.

want, and get, record salaries. In engineering, one of the fields hardest hit by unemployment, 1971 college graduates who do find jobs can expect to receive salaries slightly above those offered to the previous year's graduating class.[8]

Erosion of 'Organization Man' Outlook in Sixties

The new executive is also not moved by admonitions that life in a corporation is a 24-hour-a-day engagement which carries with it priority over family life, privacy, and any impulse to deviate from the Puritan ethic. *Business Week* reported, Feb. 7, 1970: "The prosperity of the Sixties has created a new breed of Organization Man, who places his own interests and those of his family ahead of those of the corporation. Surrounded on all sides by examples of job mobility, from job-hopping MBAs[9] to office-switching top managers, today's executive can easily believe there is always an alternative open."

In the past, the tentacles of the corporate octopus extended so far as to limit an executive's promotion potential if his wife detracted from the corporation's image in the community or if the executive's marital life was open to criticism. A change in this situation, in the automobile industry, was described Feb. 15, 1970, in a *New York Times* news dispatch from Detroit:

> One thing that has become more noticeable is an increased tolerance about the private lives of auto executives. Divorce had been generally considered to mean an end to a man's progress in auto companies....But that view began to change in 1966 when Henry Ford 2nd married Christina Austin and the change was accelerated when Roy D. Chapin Jr., board chairman of American Motors, married the former Louise Wickser and Mr. [Edward] Cole [president of General Motors] took Dollie Ann McVey as his second wife.

Another area in which the life style of new executives is eroding corporate mores is personal grooming. As recently as 1967, Clarence B. Randall wrote: "For the businessman a shave and a haircut are still evidence of good breeding."[10] By 1970, however, a college recruitment officer of the Mobil Oil Co. said: "We don't care whether they wear beards and long hair. It's what's inside them that counts."

---

[8] As reported by *U.S. News & World Report,* Dec. 21, 1970, engineering graduates could expect an average starting salary of $10,620 a year; the magazine reported March 9, 1970, that the 1970 average starting salary would be $10,465.

[9] Holders of masters' degrees in business administration.

[10] Clarence B. Randall (retired board chairman of Inland Steel Co.), *The Executive in Transition* (1967), p. 97.

Dr. E. G. Shuster, an executive of University Computing Co., McLean, Va., wrote in the August 1970 issue of *Nation's Business:* "A managerial revolution is in the making. It will largely put an end to the organization man of today. In his place, it will usher in a new type of individualist. He won't be a swashbuckling buccaneer, who allows neither codes nor conscience to stand in the way of his single-minded objectives. The new individualist will be one who combines personal freedom with professional managerial responsibility."

Evolution of U.S. Business Attitudes

ALEXIS DE TOCQUEVILLE wrote, in *Democracy in America* (1835): "Americans of all ages, all conditions, and all dispositions constantly form associations. They have not only commercial and manufacturing companies...but associations of a thousand other kinds...to give entertainments, to found seminaries, to build inns, to construct churches, to diffuse books, to send missionaries to the antipodes." Those associations of the 19th century, formed for profit and other objectives, were generally the lengthened shadow of a man. Often that man had risen "from rags to riches" by dint of daring, perseverance, thrift, and business acumen, with an admixture of practices disapproved then and now.

Matthew Josephson has described the period after the Civil War as "the paradise of freebooting capitalists, untrammeled and untaxed." This "small class of *parvenus,*" he wrote, "accepted no ethics of business conduct."[11] Collis P. Huntington, developer of the Chesapeake & Ohio Railroad, commented in 1877 on his bribery of congressmen, "If you have to pay money to have the right thing done, it is only just and fair to do it." William H. Vanderbilt, when criticized in 1882 for managing one of his railroads without regard for public service, told a newsman: "The public be damned! I am working for my stockholders." J. P. Morgan, blamed for bringing on a panic in the 1890s, said, "I owe the public nothing."

Other entrepreneurs parlayed small investments into millions by cornering markets, wiping out competitors, bribing

---

[11] Matthew Josephson, preface to the 1962 edition of his book *The Robber Barons* (originally published 1934), pp. v-vi.

officials, manipulating stock, or oppressing labor. Cornelius Vanderbilt made fortunes in railroads and shipping, Jay Gould in leather, railroads and gold, John D. Rockefeller in oil, Philip D. Armour and Gustavus F. Swift in meat-packing, Edward H. Harriman in railroads, and Elbert H. Gary in steel. Among operators of the same period and later whose names convey a more palatable flavor now are Jay Cooke, finance; Chauncey M. Depew and Russell Sage, railroads; and Andrew Carnegie, Henry C. Frick, and Charles M. Schwab, steel. Referring to the Fords, Mellons, Vanderbilts, and Rockefellers, historian Charles A. Beard likened the dynastic families founded by such "kings" of finance and industry to the ducal families of feudal England.

Today's evaluation of the wheeler-dealers of the 19th and early 20th centuries is ambivalent. Their profiteering in the Civil War, bribery, plundering of resources, conspiracies in restraint of competition, and exploitation of unorganized workers are condemned. Their vigor in opening the West and their contribution to America's emergence as an industrial power leaven the condemnation. Clarance B. Randall wrote:

> Their vision and their courage, though tinged at times with avarice, were precisely what our country needed. They had weaknesses that would not be forgiven nowadays, but for these the mores of their day were more to blame than their own personal standards. If these men had been born much later, and were active in business in our era, I am convinced they would accept our ways and conform willingly to the prevailing modes of conduct. And they would still be giants.

The philanthropies to which many buccaneers of business turned their attention after they had gained their millions put some of them in a class with Maecenas and the Medicis as patrons of learning and art. The major foundations, Ford, Rockefeller and Carnegie among others, were established by yesterday's giants whose fortunes have been turned to social betterment.

Stirrings of Corporate Soul in Muckraking Era

The harshness of capitalism operating with virtually no regulation gave way, under goading by reformers at the turn of the century, to the concept of responsible business enterprise. As noted by Virginia Carabillo, "The first stirrings of corporate soul were stimulated between 1902 and 1911 by the muckrakers such as Lincoln Steffens, Ida Tarbell, Ray Stannard Baker and Mark Sullivan who made both a science and an art of the exposure of corruption in business and government."[12] Upton Sinclair's novel *The Jungle* (1906) aroused indignation over unsanitary and anti-labor features of the meat-packing industry. Edwin Markham inveighed against the employment of child labor. Louis D. Brandeis criticized the excessive profits Massachusetts life insurance companies made at the expense of factory workers.

The impact of the muckrakers was beneficial but limited in scope. Prodded by the furor set off by *The Jungle,* Congress in 1906 passed a Food and Drug Act and the next

---

[12] Virginia Carabillo, "The Corporate Search for Soul," *SDC* (System Development Corp.) *Magazine,* fall 1969, p. 2. Theodore Roosevelt chose the occasion of dedicating an office building of the House of Representatives, April 14, 1906, to denounce reform journalists for attacking the character of Chauncey M. Depew, a railroad magnate. He called them "muckrakers" on the basis of a passage in John Bunyan's *Pilgrim's Progress.* The new word was adopted by defenders and critics of the reform movement.

year a Meat Inspection Act, but the marketing of adulterated, substandard and misbranded meats continued through various legal loopholes.[13] The Child Labor Law was still a decade away (1916) and collective bargaining with employers would remain on unsure legal ground until the coming of the New Deal.

The Sherman Antitrust Act of 1890, which outlawed monopolization of any part of U.S. trade, was largely ignored or circumvented at first. But it began to be seriously enforced under President Theodore Roosevelt, whose "trustbusting" fervor led to Supreme Court decisions in 1911 requiring the breakup of oil and tobacco monopolies and then to the Clayton Act of 1914, which banned business actions aimed at lessening competition.[14]

Industrial companies became more accountable for distribution of their surpluses, and some industrial companies, especially in steel, gave their employees shares of stock as bonuses when business was good. But ethical standards in the dealings of business concerns with one another, with government, and with the public remained at a low level.

Rise of New Class of Professional Executives

Two related developments in the 20th century have modified the operation of corporations: the growing size of corporations and the growing separation of ownership from management. Beginning soon after World War I, millions of Americans eagerly bought stock in corporations,[15] which were turning to Wall Street for the financing of their expansion. The diffusion of ownership of a big corporation left the management of it in the hands of a group of paid officials and a pyramid of subordinate executives.

This turn of events has been the subject of extensive critical analysis. One line of criticism draws on Adam Smith's expression, in *The Wealth of Nations* (1776), that "managers of other people's money...cannot well be expected...to watch over it with the same anxious vigilance" as the owners would. Concern from another angle was voiced by a German social historian, who said "the depersonalization of ownership...leads

---

[13] See "Food Additives," *E.R.R.*, 1969 Vol. II, pp. 966-967.

[14] See "Business Concentration and Antitrust Laws," *E.R.R.*, 1966 Vol. I, pp. 388-389.

[15] The number of stockholders has steadily grown. It is estimated that today 26 million Americans own stock directly and 100 million others do indirectly, through pension funds and in other ways. See "Wall Street: 40 Years After the Crash," *E.R.R.*, 1969 Vol. II, p. 755.

to a point where the enterprise becomes transformed into an institution which resembles the state in character."[16] Adolf A. Berle Jr. and Gardiner C. Means, in their classic study *The Modern Corporation and Private Property* (1932), raised the question, without answering it, by what moral right management governs business without bearing the risk of losses.

Since 1932, when their study was made, the tendency toward managerial control has continued, as has the dispersion of stockholding. James Burnham, an ex-Trotskyite turned conservative, contended in 1941 that the United States had entered a period of transition between a time when the bourgeoisie was the dominant class and a future era when the managers "will be the dominant or ruling class."[17]

A decade and a half later, William H. Whyte pointed out that executives obsessed with their organization are found not only in business. "Blood brother to the business trainee off to join Du Pont," he wrote, "is the seminary student who will end up in the church hierarchy, the doctor headed for the corporate clinic, the physics Ph.D. in a government laboratory, the intellectual on the foundation-sponsored team project, the engineering graduate in the huge drafting room at Lockheed, the young apprentice in a Wall Street law factory." The fault, he said, "is not in organization...it is in our worship of it."[18]

Students of the Soviet Union report that the organization man exists there also. A revealing account of the Russian managerial ladder and its climbers was provided in 1960 by David Granick, a professor at the Carnegie Institute of Technology, in his book *The Red Executive: A Study of the Organization Man in Russia.* Further studies, by others, have portrayed the "technocrat" in charge of the governmental apparatus in the Soviet Union and the corporate state in America.

The authors of a spoof on corporation executives concluded that "in a hierarchy every employee tends to rise to his level of incompetence" (the Peter principle), with the result that large organizations have numerous senior managers who are not able to do the job to which they were promoted.[19] Robert

---

[16] Walter Rathenau, *In Days to Come* (1921, translated by Eden and Cedar Paul), p. 121.
[17] James Burnham, *The Managerial Revolution* (new edition, 1960), p. 74.
[18] William H. Whyte, *The Organization Man* (1956), pp. 3, 13.
[19] Laurence J. Peter and Raymond Hull, *The Peter Principle* (1969).

Townsend, a former business executive (Avis), struck a similar note in his best-selling book, *Up the Organization* (1970). Townsend advised operating executives to stick to making operating decisions. To free themselves for this work, they should fire their secretaries, delegate responsibility not to the next lower level but all the way down to the man who has the necessary know-how, divert boards of directors from making serious suggestions, encourage subordinates when they make mistakes— "that's how they grow"—and shunt protocol calls and complaints to a clerk designated as Chairman of the Executive Committee.

Impact of White-Collar Crime on Business Image

It is impossible to say exactly when the public began to view the organization man as having tunnel vision. Some social historians believe that the Depression Thirties blemished the image of American business for all time. Others argue that in the 1950s business was as high in public esteem as in the booming 1920s, when President Coolidge reportedly said "the business of America is business."[20] It is generally agreed that the public picture of business began to tarnish once again in the 1960s, a decade in which few institutions were spared. The reasons may be found in many places, including the youth revolt with its anti-establishment flavor and the growing public awareness of the dangers of industrial pollution. White-collar crime may well be another reason.

In the popular view of the organization man, he devoted his energies to the company's interests as a channel for his own advancement. Ethics supposedly did not enter into the considerations determining his corporate mentality and behavior. If an opportunity arose by which the company's profits could be increased in a legally questionable deal, the organization man seized the opportunity. That, at least, was the sterotype of the organization man.

Violations of the law by corporations, instigated by scheming executives, came to be called white-collar crime. Business departures from legality often were condoned as an almost unavoidable feature of the adulation of what William James had called the "bitch-goddess, Success." A study of 70 large U.S. industrial corporations during 15 years (1934-49) showed that 60 per cent of them had been convicted of

---

[20] What he actually said is in dispute. According to some accounts, the phrase he used in a speech to the Society of American Newspaper Editors, Jan. 17, 1925, was: "The business of business is business."

violations and that the average number of convictions for a corporation that had any at all was four.[21]

On Dec. 8, 1960, General Electric, Westinghouse, and 27 other electrical equipment companies, and certain of their top officers, pleaded guilty or *nolo contendere* (no contest) in the federal district court at Philadelphia to charges of collusive price-fixing and bid-rigging. Judge J. Cullen Ganey on Feb. 6-7, 1961, sentenced seven of the company officials to jail for 30 days for violation of the Sherman Act, gave suspended 30-day jail sentences to 23 others, putting them on probation for five years, and imposed fines totaling $137,500 on 44 officials of 29 companies and $1,787,000 on the companies.[22]

The federal government and various utility companies filed suits against the convicted companies for damages running to millions of dollars.[23] The American Management Association, planning a meeting in New York in 1961 on ethics in business, could not find a business leader willing to speak on the topic. Thirty executives declined the invitation. Public antipathy for white-collar crime received further impetus when Ralph Nader set out on his crusade against corporations that put profit ahead of public service.

Coming Decisions for Executive Suites

BUCKMINSTER FULLER refers to the pace of change as "the acceleration of acceleration." In the opinion of some management development professionals, executives who want to keep their knowledge current in a period of swift and frequent change will need to spend as much as 10 per cent of their time in campus-like centers for executive education, conducted by companies or groups of companies. These executive centers "will be slightly subversive," according to Kenneth

---

[21]Edwin H. Sutherland, *White Collar Crime* (new edition, 1961).

[22] The fine imposed on General Electric was $437,500; on Westinghouse, $372,500. See "Business Morality," *E.R.R.*, 1961 Vol. I, pp. 401-402.

[23] The federal government over a period of years received $8,918,650 in damages as a result of these suits. Among the large awards to utility companies was one of Aug. 31, 1965, amounting to almost $17 million to be paid by General Electric and Westinghouse to the Ohio Valley Electric Corp. and its subsidiary, the Indiana-Kentucky Electric Corp.

Andrews, professor at the Harvard Graduate School of Business Administration, because "executives will be taught to challenge corporate policy as a way of life."

Self-renewal is easier for executives with extensive academic training, since they are accustomed to concentrated study, fact-finding, and analysis and appraisal of raw data. Of executives in big business, the proportion with college training rose from 39 per cent in 1900 to 76 per cent in 1950, both figures being 10 times the proportion of college men of their age groups in the total population. The Du Pont Co. in 1967 had nearly 2,500 Ph.D.'s on the payroll, a number that few universities could match.

Issue of Accountability: Stockholders or Public

Re-education of those immersed in corporate life will deepen their awareness of the tug between accountability for profit and obligations to the public. The following report on the new gospel of business responsibility was written almost two decades ago but might well have been written in 1971:

> Only within the past few years...have large numbers of business leaders publicly acknowledged and actively preached the doctrine that they are servants of society and that management merely in the interests (narrowly defined) of stockholders is not the sole end of their duties. Indeed, discussion of the "social responsibilities of business" has become not only acceptable in leading business circles, but even fashionable.[24]

Michael Harrington, author of *The Other America: Poverty in America* (1962), has cast doubt on the genuineness of the new business philosophy. Businessmen, he wrote, have "acquired a conscience at the precise moment when...there is money to be made in doing good." An even more skeptical view was expressed by David Finn, who wrote:

> The mountain of recent speeches, articles and reports describing the new sense of corporate responsibility in top-management circles rests on very insecure grounds indeed. Executives are saying many self-flattering things about their new corporate goals, and many claim to be making a serious effort to devote corporate resources and their own time to support non-profit-oriented causes. But...the corporate oligarch talks about saving American society from destruction *lest the corporation itself be destroyed in the process!* [Finn's italics] This hardly represents a change in priorities....Corporate power...is still considered the end and social action the means to that end, instead of vice versa.[25]

---

[24] Howard Bowen, *Social Responsibilities of the Businessman* (1953), p. 44.

[25] David Finn, *The Corporate Oligarch* (1969), pp. 246-247.

Sponsors and opponents of the new business view have traded the epithet "unrealistic." Initially, Paul T. Heyne wrote that "leading business spokesmen" have rejected the older business doctrine of profit first as "outmoded and unrealistic."[26] Then, Peter F. Drucker described the "new demand" and "new expectations" as being "dangerously unrealistic."[27] Milton Friedman has used even stronger language: "Few trends could so thoroughly undermine the very foundations of our free society as the acceptance by corporate officials of a social responsibility other than to make as much money for their stockholders as possible."[28]

The U.S. Chamber of Commerce on March 9, 1970, took action which, if Friedman's words are taken literally, would fall within his category of actions undermining the foundations of our free society. The Chamber issued a code for businessmen's and manufacturers' relations with consumers. Recommended in the code are protection of human safety in the design and manufacture of products, elimination of falsity in advertising, simplification of guarantees, improvement of services, and setting of fair prices for servicing.

The National Association of Manufacturers has also been confounding its old friends and critics, particularly the latter who long have regarded it as the nation's strongest voice for reactionary capitalism. Murray Seeger of the *Los Angeles Times* wrote in advance of the NAM's 75th anniversary meeting in New York in December 1970: "Probably the most symbolic event in marking the changed outlook of the NAM was its decision to support President Nixon's proposal to replace the nation's much-criticized public welfare system with a broadly based Family Assistance Plan. This decision put the NAM in the unusual position of opposing the United States Chamber of Commerce." Seeger reported "the low point for the NAM came in the late 1950s when public figures began to shun the organization for fear of being marked reactionary." Since 1962, he added, the NAM has moved from the far right on issues toward the middle of the road.

---

[26] Paul T. Heyne (associate professor of economics, Southern Methodist University), *Private Keepers of the Public Interest* (1968), p. 3.

[27] Peter F. Drucker, "Business and the Quality of Life," in Drucker (ed.), *Preparing Tomorrow's Business Leaders Today* (1969), p. 77. Drucker holds that government, labor, and non-profit organizations, along with business, are responsible for the quality of life.

[28] Milton Friedman, *Capitalism and Freedom* (1962), p. 133. Friedman has restated the thought at various times. He is willing for corporations to be taxed to help finance a guaranteed income. See "Guaranteed Income Plan," *E.R.R.*, 1966 Vol. I, p. 404.

Business efforts to aid the poor include such undertakings as those promoted by the National Alliance of Businessmen, which in 1968-70 found jobs for 387,000 of the hard-core unemployed. Life insurance companies have pledged an investment of $1 billion in urban renewal, with hoped-for amelioration of problems of the cities; Control Data Corp. opened plants in the black slums of Washington, D.C., and Minneapolis; Detroit's auto makers took on tens of thousands of jobless poor in a massive re-training project.

Role of Executives in Promoting Social Reform

Peter F. Drucker a number of years ago struck a cautionary note on involvement of business leaders in agitation for reform. He collected a dossier of news accounts, for a single month, of activities of top businessmen in conservation, freedom of the press, employment of the handicapped, and other causes. "You might wonder," he wrote, "if you were a conscientious newspaper reader, when the managers of American business had any time for business."[29]

The alliance of business with government in improving conditions of life for all is beginning to create new problems while promoting solution of old ones. Maintenance of public control over complex business operations in the field of social betterment will be, at best, difficult. To the question "Is the American system of government up to the challenge?" Richard J. Barber's answer is: "A realist cannot be other than pessimistic." If the government does not equip itself to guide their direction, he wrote, "the big industrial corporations will pretty much shape tomorrow's world, in their own image and without the guidance that democratic government should provide."[30] But the government, with the cooperation of a new generation of executives and professionals, can equip itself to provide the necessary guidance.

Barber also contends that "by the mid-1970s social problem solving will be one of the biggest new industries in the United States." Such a development would entail, among other things, the transfer of skills that have been acquired in handling the problems of defense and space exploration to civilian areas which only now are beginning to receive the full amount

---

[29] Peter F. Drucker, "The Responsibilities of Management," *Harper's Magazine,* November 1954, p. 67.

[30] Richard J. Barber (former counsel of the Senate Antitrust and Monopoly Subcommittee), *The American Corporation; Its Power, Its Money, Its Politics* (1970), pp. 293-294.

of public attention they have long been denied. Instead of making aircraft or shoes, a company may turn to solving problems in education, transportation, medical care, law enforcement, housing city renewal—all for profit.

But the problems are as complex and difficult as the potential is large. "What makes the challenge to business even more difficult is that these problems are intrinsically political in nature," Barber added, "necessitating substantial government involvement and compelling industrial firms to contest with issues that are beyond their established expertise."

> The problems...are not susceptible...to objective definition and resolution. They can be ultimately resolved only with public participation and it is this fact which means that business must accept government as a partner, working out accommodations as their efforts proceed. This sounds good in theory, but whether it can or will work in practice is open to serious question.

There is also the question of whether tommorow's students will view a social-industrial complex with any less abhorrence than today's students view the so-called military-industrial complex. There is one sign of possible change in the future corporate world, however, that may be to the liking of the youth generation. It is that corporations, after years of expansion, are beginning to find some virtue in smallness. Dean S. Ammer, director of the Bureau of Business and Economic Research at Northwestern University, recently noted that the profitability of big concerns is tending to lag behind that of smaller ones—a reversal of past experience.

Writing in the December 1970 issue of *Business Management,* Ammer said the advantages of big business are no longer sufficient to offset its inflexibility. A big company maintains controls that permit it to operate efficiently but inhibit innovation. Thus, he added, it maintains an autocratic image that discourages young, adventurous talent. "Several top executives I interviewed agreed that the first to feel stifled in the big company environment are those recent graduates the company would most like to keep." It might be one of the ironies of the 1970s that big business and young people will come to a meeting of the minds on this matter, though for entirely different reasons.

TECHNOLOGY LAG IN AMERICA

by

Ralph C. Deans

CONCERN OVER STATUS OF U.S. TECHNOLOGY
Fear of Slippage in U.S. Superiority; Nixon Plan
Criticism of Stress on Arms and Space Research
Controversy Over Technology's Impact on Trade
Questions About R & D; Areas of Lag in Technology

FEDERAL SUPPORT FOR SCIENCE ACTIVITY
Beginnings of Public Spending on Technical Goals
Funding of Research in World War II and Later
Spurt in Space Activities After Sputnik Flights
Cutbacks in University and Industrial Research

DIRECTIONS FOR TECHNOLOGY IN SEVENTIES
Issues of Pollution Control and Science Priorities
Debate Over Support for Basic or Applied Research
Sharing of Federally Acquired Data With Business

**1 9 7 2
Jan. 5**

TECHNOLOGY LAG IN AMERICA

AMERICAN LEADERSHIP in science and technology has been accepted almost without question since World War II. Salk vaccine, the digital computer and the moon landings are proof of the scope and vitality of research and development in the United States. Yet the argument is growing that the U.S. leadership is slipping away, jeopardizing American trade and prestige abroad. There is now a broadly based effort, centered in the White House, to revitalize the research establishment. President Nixon has promised to recommend "new tax proposals for stimulating research and development of new industries and technologies" this month, possibly in his State of the Union address to Congress. The President stressed the need for greater research in his economics statement of Aug. 15.[1] After the return of the Apollo 15 astronauts, Nixon told Congress Sept. 9 that "the remarkable technology that took these Americans to the moon can be applied to reaching our goals here on Earth." Business technology will be one of four major topics discussed at a White House Conference on The Industrial World Ahead, planned for Feb. 9-11.

To coordinate the effort, Nixon appointed William Magruder, formerly manager of the Supersonic Transport project, as a special consultant in charge of the New Technology Opportunities Program. John Pierson, writing in *The Wall Street Journal* of Dec. 14, 1971, said the program "could become the centerpiece of Mr. Nixon's election-year domestic strategy." Still under study is how government will promote scientific endeavor—whether through tax cuts, loans, grants, or cost-sharing proposals.

Debate on a science policy has been sharpened in recent months with concern over the nation's first deficit since 1893 in its foreign trade—$1.7 billion for the first 11 months of 1971. There is also concern over slow economic growth and heavy unemployment among scientists and engineers. Nicholas Wade of *Science* magazine believes these factors will probably lead to "a significant effort by the administration to invigorate the

---

[1] In which he announced a wage-price freeze and a suspension of the dollar's convertibility into gold. See "World Money Crisis," *E.R.R.*, 1971 Vol. II, p. 693.

national R & D [research and development] enterprise" during 1972.[2] According to many observers, it is high time that something was done.

Emilio Q. Daddario, in an interview published in *Forbes* magazine, Nov. 15, 1971, said "our very existence as a free nation is at stake" if America loses its position as world leader in science.[3] Others take a vastly different view. Technology is being accused of debasing the quality of life, causing pollution and dehumanizing the environment. Social critic Paul Goodman notes that some dissident young people feel that "science is anti-life...and scientific technology has manifestly become diabolical."[4] That view was echoed, at least in part, by a special panel of the National Academy of Sciences which recommended the creation of a new agency, close to the center of political power, to alert the nation to the perils of uncontrolled applications of science.[5]

Whatever the moral, ethical and philosophic doubts, the "science problem" boils down to a series of basic questions: Will more technology clean up the environment and improve the quality of life or worsen it? Since "high-technology" items are vital elements in foreign trade, does the United States face a continued balance-of-trade deficit unless it invests ever more heavily in research and development? Should the nation's major scientific effort emphasize basic research or the resolution of specific problems? And if R & D expenditures are to be increased, who will bear the cost?

Criticism of Emphasis on Arms and Space Research

Concern about the health of American technology came as a surprise to many Europeans who thought they were the ones suffering from a technology gap. The Organization for Economic Cooperation and Development (OECD) reported in November 1965 that American spending on R & D was four times greater than in all the major West European states combined.[6] Those statistics are believed to be still valid. The research and development enterprise in the United States is

---

[2] Nicholas Wade, "Nixon's New Economic Policy: Hints of a Resurgence for R & D," *Science*, Aug. 27, 1971, p. 794.

[3] Daddario, now senior vice president of Gulf & Western Precision Engineering, is a former chairman of the House Subcommittee on Science, Research and Development, a unit of the Committee on Science and Astronautics.

[4] Paul Goodman, "The New Reformation," *The New York Times Magazine*, Sept. 14, 1969, p. 33. Also see "Science and Society," *E.R.R.*, 1969 Vol. II, pp. 775-776.

[5] National Academy of Sciences, *Technology: Processes of Assessment and Choice* (1969), p. 1.

[6] OECD, *The R & D Effor in Western Europe, North America and the Soviet Union* (1965).

so huge and diffuse that its size can only be guessed at. Estimates of total spending for R & D in the past year vary from $26.9 billion to $28 billion—roughly 2.6 per cent of the gross national product. The research and development "industry" employs more than one million persons in 17,000 establishments—government agencies, private firms, universities and industrial departments.

It is not the size of the research effort that worries some Americans. They contend that comparisons between the research expenditures of the United States and other countries must take account of the high priority that is given American military and space technology. The National Science Foundation has estimated that fully three-quarters of all federal funding of research is devoted to military and space projects. And federal funds account for the lion's share of the total spent on research in the United States. President Nixon's budget requests for R & D in fiscal 1972 totaled a relatively austere $16.7 billion and it has been estimated that $14.8 billion will be spent—slightly more than the $14.7 billion spent in 1970.

It is frequently argued that military research is essentially non-productive—that it does not normally increase industrial productivity or add to the stock of usable products in the civilian economy. While there is some spillover of military technology into the civilian economy, the amount is difficult to assess and generally held to be slight. "There are jet aircraft, nuclear reactors, computers and after that there's trivia," according to Seymour Melman, professor of industrial engineering and management at Columbia University.

Once the expenditures for defense-related research are subtracted, the "technology gap" is sharply narrowed. Furthermore, it is argued that the research dollar goes farther on the other side of the Atlantic. "When research and development efforts are translated into cost-equivalent terms...the relative advantage of the United States investment in civilian research and development disappears," according to J. Herbert Hollomon of the Massachusetts Institute of Technology and his assistant, Alan E. Harger.[7]

Melman believes the defense effort has turned the universities into training centers for the Department of Defense and

---

[7] Hollomon and Harger, "America's Technological Dilemma," *Technology Review*, July-August 1971, p. 38. Hollomon, consultant to the president of MIT, served as Assistant Secretary of Commerce for science and technology under Presidents Kennedy and Johnson. He previously spent 16 years with General Electric.

the National Aeronautics and Space Administration—developing "vast numbers of men with the trained incapacity to work in civilian industry." Dr. Edward E. David Jr., President Nixon's chief science adviser, disagrees. "There's no real limitation, other than people's attitudes, standing in the way of their conversion to civilian employment," he said. "There is, I think we have to admit, some reluctance on the part of traditional industry to take these people on, because they say— quite falsely I believe—that the aerospace people are not conditioned to look at the costs and benefits in the way *they* look at them."[8]

The cutbacks in government-sponsored research—due in part to the burden of the Viet Nam War and resulting attempts to contain the growth of the federal budget—have thrown thousands of scientists and engineers out of work. David has estimated the number of unemployed scientists and engineers at 50,000 but other estimates have run twice as high. Among other things, "Layoffs of scientists and engineers have caused many Europeans who were part of the original brain drain to the United States to return to Europe, and an increasing number of American scientists to move abroad."[9]

Controversy Over Technology's Impact on Trade

The "technology lag" issue came to public attention in March 1971 when Congress canceled further federal participation in a project to build a supersonic transport plane for commercial purposes. The vote, together with a Senate defeat May 19 of a House attempt to revive the SST, was cheered by environmentalists but decried by those who argued that this nation was deliberately choosing to forfeit its pre-eminence in air transportation.

Official concern about a lag in technology arose earlier, much of it stemming from an analysis made by Michael T. Boretsky, 50, a senior policy analyst in the Department of Commerce. Boretsky did not indicate that the United States had fallen behind other nations technologically. But he did conclude that the industrial and technological capabilities of Western Europe, Japan and Canada were growing at a faster *rate* than those of the United States, and he warned that unless something was done the United States would lose its lead. According to Boretsky, more than national prestige was involved.

---

[8] Melman and David were quoted by Robert Nash in *Forbes*, Nov. 15, 1971.

[9] Henry R. Nau, "A Political Interpretation of the Technology Gap Dispute," *Orbis*, Summer 1971, p. 542. Also see "Unemployment in Recessions," *E.R.R.*, 1970 Vol. II, pp. 941-942.

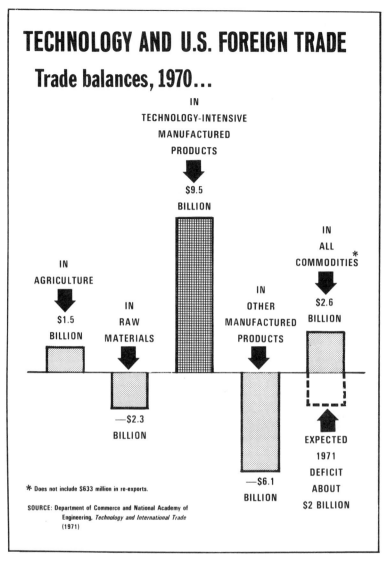

TECHNOLOGY AND U.S. FOREIGN TRADE
Trade balances, 1970...

IN
TECHNOLOGY-INTENSIVE
MANUFACTURED
PRODUCTS

$9.5
BILLION

IN
ALL
COMMODITIES *

IN
AGRICULTURE

IN
OTHER
MANUFACTURED
PRODUCTS

$2.6
BILLION

$1.5
BILLION

IN
RAW
MATERIALS

—$2.3
BILLION

—$6.1
BILLION

EXPECTED
1971
DEFICIT
ABOUT
$2 BILLION

* Does not include $633 million in re-exports.

SOURCE: Department of Commerce and National Academy of
Engineering, *Technology and International Trade*
(1971)

In a paper he delivered to the National Academy of Engineering in October 1970,[10] Boretsky said that American competitiveness in world trade had been maintained only by the country's ability to sell "high technology" (or "technology intensive") products such as aircraft, computers and chemicals. A trade surplus in these "big ticket" items, he said, masked a widening deficit in two other major categories—raw

---

[10] The paper, "Concerns About the Present American Position in International Trade," was published in an Academy publication, *Technology and Trade* (1971).

EXPORTS OF HIGH TECHNOLOGY ITEMS

Item	1970 Exports (millions)	Comparison of Growth Rates	
		1970 to 1969 (per cent)	Avg. per year 1962 - 1969 (per cent)
Chemicals	$3,826	+ 13	+ 9
Non-electrical machinery	8,677	+ 16	+ 9
Metalworking machine tools	305	+ 21	− 3
Electrical machines and apparatus	3,000	+ 12	+ 10
Scientific and Professional instruments and controls	857	+ 9	+ 15
Aircraft and parts	2,658	+ 10	+ 17
Motor vehicles and parts	3,244	− 8	+ 15

materials and "low technology" goods such as textiles and footwear.[11] Peter G. Peterson, a presidential adviser on international economic policy, told newsmen at a year-end briefing, Dec. 30, 1971: "We now see the picture on so-called technology intensive products and...how dependent we have become on these products for export." They "are well over half of the total and we have a positive balance here of about... $8 billion or roughly the magnitude of the deficit on the non-technology intensive products."

While there had long been fretfulness about the impact of technology on trade, many economists believed that the dwindling trade balance was due chiefly to inflationary pressures which drove up the price of American goods on world markets. Boretsky's findings indicated, however, that the trade problem began to emerge long before inflation was first detected in the mid-1960s. According to science writer Philip M. Boffey, "It is probably not fair to say that Boretsky is personally responsible for the crescendo of alarm. But it is fair to say that many of those who have publicly expressed concern over America's technological leadership have leaned heavily on Boretsky to prove their point."[12]

Using Boretsky's findings, many government spokesmen have made a strong call for an increase in R & D expenditures.

---

[11] Agriculture, the fourth major category of American foreign trade, has shown a steady but slight surplus over the years. See "Competition for World Markets," *E.R.R.,* 1970 Vol. II, pp. 589-606.

[12] Philip M. Boffey, "Technology and World Trade: Is There Cause for Alarm?" *Science,* April 2, 1971, p. 38.

But Lester C. Thurow, professor of economics at Massachusetts Institute of Technology, questions whether such expenditures really help the trade picture. "While it may seem almost axiomatic that more research and development activities should lead to more technical progress," Thurow wrote, "it is difficult to postulate this axiom on the basis of American history since 1940. More research expenditures do not seem to lead to more technical progress."

Question About R & D; Extent of Lag in Technology

It is not the amount spent on research that concerns many critics, but the quality of the scientific effort. Paul Dickson contends that millions of dollars are being squandered. "As in any other multi-billion-dollar industry that offers the promise of a fast buck, hustlers, tycoons and those willing to sell their objectivity for a fat contract have been attracted into R & D along with the honest, hard-working researcher," he wrote.

> While abuses exist throughout the R & D empire [he continued], they are...most noticeable at the federal level. Bad research is hard to control and detect. Much of it is delivered on paper in the form of a report that can be—and often is—slipped away in a filing cabinet by the bureaucrat who commissioned it.

> Major R & D projects that do not work out are simply canceled, though in the case of the Pentagon, for example, such a showdown can add up to quite a large sum of money wasted. During the period from 1954 to 1970, some sixty-eight major weapons projects were terminated; a total of $10.7 billion was invested in them before they failed, faltered, or were canceled.[13]

The government's large role in research and development is criticized on several grounds. It is asserted that space and defense research gobbled up the best scientists and technicians; that high taxes robbed business of necessary dollars to carry on industrial research; and that anti-trust laws impeded business cooperation in research. The resulting lack of industrial research, it is added, made many American goods noncompetitive in world markets. John Kenneth Galbraith, the Harvard economist and author, finds fault in another way. "Much has been accomplished by research and development ...under the inspiration of military need," he wrote. "But this is a hideously inefficient way of subsidizing general scientific and technical development."[14]

Lawrence Lessing of *Fortune* magazine listed in March 1971 several areas in which American science and technology appear to be falling behind:

[13] Paul Dickson, *Think Tanks* (1971), pp. 39-40.
[14] John Kenneth Galbraith, *The Affluent Society* (1969), p. 316.

High-energy physics. "Europe in the late Sixties took the lead in developing so-called colliding-beam electron accelerators, the latest in Big Machines investigating the sub-atomic particles of matter."

Radio astronomy. "The U.S., after a strong surge to a leadership position in the Fifties, is rapidly losing its place.... Large advanced radio arrays have been going up in England, Germany, Holland, Russia, and even India...."

Space science. "Our present position was tersely put by Dr. George M. Low, NASA's acting administrator.... 'The U.S. leads today, but we are rapidly losing our capability that made us first.' "

Transportation. "The creation of new mass transportation systems to relieve our choking roads lags far behind—though not for lack of abundant new technology."

In steel and textiles, technological advances and export leadership have passed into foreign hands. A similar story is that of consumer electronics—radios, television sets, tape recorders and phonographs. "The U.S. was once pre-eminent in this field," *U.S. News & World Report* noted, June 7, 1971. "In 1970, however, U.S. exports totaled only 77 million dollars while imports, mostly from Japan, reached 1.2 billion.... In autos and electronics, particularly, several countries including Japan have taken advantage of lower wage costs to undercut the lead in know-how which has been held by the United States." Citing other examples as well, the magazine observed: "Suddenly, evidence is piling up on all sides that this nation no longer possesses its unchallenged across-the-board superiority of years past. Instead many experts suggest the U.S. is facing a new and critical problem: a 'technology lag.' "

Federal Support for Science Activity

THE CONSTITUTION accorded Congress the right "to promote the Progress of Science and useful Arts" [Article I, section 8] but the power was construed narrowly to mean the protection of the rights of authors and inventors. Presidents Washington, Jefferson, John Adams and Madison were "sympathetic toward the promotion of science." And while Congress was "largely indifferent" to science and "only a minority saw the advantages of an alliance between science and the federal government, that small group included some of the most influential men in public life. Science has had a place in the government continuously since 1789."[15]

---

[15] A. Hunter Dupree, *Science in the Federal Government* (1957), p. 19.

Paul Dickson has written that the heavy involvement of government in science began in 1832 when "the Secretary of the Treasury, confronted by pesky steam boilers that kept exploding on American steamboats, contracted with the Franklin Institute of Philadelphia for a study of the problem. Since then, the government has been paying for more and more outside brainpower each decade."[16] Samuel Morse wrangled $30,000 from Congress in 1843 to build a telegraph line between Washington and Baltimore. Charles G. Page obtained some federal support in 1850 for his work on the electric motor.

The Civil War led to large increases in government spending on scientific study. The Army and Navy conducted several studies related to weaponry, transportation, communications and medicine. The Smithsonian Institution, set up in 1846, also aided the war effort. Historians assert that the North's technological and industrial superiority was a major factor in winning the war. The government remained involved in scientific activity throughout the remainder of the 19th century—chiefly in agriculture, medicine, and land surveying.

Almost all governmental support of science was directed toward a specific end—such as the early grants from the War Department to develop a flying machine. Only in recent years has the government supported basic research with public funds. The Smithsonian was the only federal agency created in the 19th century devoted to the promotion of scientific endeavor. And it was a full century before the next agency devoted to science for science's sake was established—the National Science Foundation in 1947.[17]

Funding of Research in World War II and Later

World War I marked the beginning of close cooperation between government and science for military goals. This alliance was renewed and strengthened in World War II and has left its mark to this day. "Out of World War II, in what has been called the greatest mobilization of scientists and technologists in history, came a great victory...and a cornucopia of great technical developments.... From these wartime projects in due time came the antibiotics, atomic power, cryogenics,

---

[16] Paul Dickson, *op. cit.*, p. 9.

[17] Historians trace the justification of governmental support of science to a report of the National Resources Planning Board in 1938. The board defined research as a national resource and, since the government had responsibility for national resources, it became responsible for the welfare of all research establishments, both in and out of government. See *Federal Role in Research*, Vol. I of *Research—A National Resource* (1938), a report of the National Resources Planning Board.

computers, jet planes, rocket vehicles, radar, transistors, masers, lasers and other products that became the new industrial face of the mid-century."[18]

Even abstruse science, in this case theoretical physics, was enlisted in the war effort to make the atomic bomb. The bomb project, the crowning military-scientific achievement of the war, set off a wave of soul-searching among scientists which is echoed to this day. Their self-questioning as to the scientist's proper role in society set forth many of the arguments since heard over what the nation's science policy should be. Among other things, a group of the atomic physicists persuaded Congress to create a civilian Atomic Energy Commission.

As the war drew to a close, President Roosevelt requested Dr. Vannevar Bush to study the direction that science should take in peacetime. Bush, who had directed the wartime scientific effort, soon issued his famous report, *Science, the Endless Frontier* (1945). It recommended a National Science Foundation backed by public funds to support basic science. Congress debated his proposal at length and when a bill finally reached President Truman in 1947 he vetoed it, contending that it lacked proper government control. NSF came into existence three years later when Truman's differences with Congress on this matter were compromised. In approving the NSF charter, Truman expressed a philosophy which continues to be the dominant impulse behind governmental support of science:

> We have come to know that our ability to survive and grow as a nation depends to a very large degree upon our scientific progress. Moreover, it is not enough simply to keep abreast of the rest of the world in scientific matters. We must maintain our leadership. [19]

The period between 1950 and 1957 was a relatively calm one. But if there was less talk about science and science policy, "there was a steady if not spectacular growth in federal research and development activity." [20] Due to the Korean War, the Cold War and competition with the Russians in military missilery, the principal source of science funding was the Department of Defense. Many scientists turned to it for money to carry on basic research unrelated to military applications. The National Science Foundation was partially eclipsed during this period, and its role as a

[18] Lawrence Lessing, "The Senseless War on Science," *Fortune*, March 1971, p. 91.

[19] *Public Papers of the Presidents,* Harry S. Truman, 1950, pp. 369-370.

[20] Report of the House Subcommittee on Science, Research and Development, *Toward a Science Policy for the United States* (1970), p. 88.

DIVISION OF ALL R & D FUNDS*

Year	Defense-Space	All others	Year	Defense-Space	All others
1960	54.7%	45.3%	1966	51.7%	48.3%
1961	54.7	45.3	1967	49.7	50.3
1962	53.4	46.6	1968	47.8	52.2
1963	54.9	45.1	1969 (prel.)	45.2	54.8
1964	55.7	44.3	1970 (est.)	42.1	57.9
1965	53.6	46.4	1971 (est.)	39.0	61.0

*Government, industrial and others.
SOURCE: National Science Foundation.

---

coordinating and advisory body was further diminished during the space race which followed.

Spurt in Space Research After Sputnik Flights

The space age began in earnest on Oct. 4, 1957, when the Soviet Union succeeded in orbiting Sputnik I, a satellite both larger and heavier than any being built then by the United States. There was consternation in Congress and in military circles. Frequently, no distinction was drawn between Soviet space and military efforts. "For a few weeks Mr. Eisenhower was able to resist the clamor for action," Edwin Diamond wrote. "But little by little he capitulated. On Nov. 27, 1957, both the Army Jupiter and Air Force Thor—two overlapping medium-range missiles which had been competing for survival—were *both* ordered into production. The panic button was also pressed for more long-range missiles."

On Dec. 9, 1957, the Polaris submarine program was accelerated. So were the Atlas and Titan ICBM programs, also overlapping projects; the Minuteman ICBM program was stepped up. Thus, not one but four long-range nuclear delivery systems capable of reaching the Soviet Union were being pushed to close the "gap" that was to appear in the early 1960s. [21]

Soon after Sputnik went aloft, Eisenhower created the Office of Special Assistant to the President for Science and Technology. He named Dr. James R. Killian, president of Massachusetts Institute of Technology, to this position. The President also enlarged and reconstituted the former Science Advisory Committee of the Office of Defense Mobilization as the President's Science Advisory Committee, and named Killian to head it. The following year, 1959, Eisenhower created the Federal Council for Science and Technology— an intra-agency coordinating committee in the White House. For the first time, a scientific agency had its home in the White House.

---

[21] Edwin Diamond, *The Rise and Fall of the Space Age* (1964), p. 26.

Congress soon created several new committees to guide the growing national commitment to space activity and a civilian agency, NASA, to administer the principal parts of the space program. In the interests of "catching up with the Russians," Congress broadened the scope of spending to several areas of science, including grants to universities to promote the output of science and engineering graduates. Funds for such purposes multiplied. NASA's budget doubled yearly, reaching $5 billion in 1965. Much of the growth reflected Congress's endorsement of President Kennedy's call in 1961 for a manned moon landing "before the decade is out."

By the time Neil A. Armstrong became the first man to set foot on the moon, July 20, 1969, space spending had fallen into decline and space objectives were being questioned in Congress, the press and the scientific community. In fact, all of science and technology had been swept from its pinnacle of public esteem by the social unrest that grew as the decade advanced. Space and defense spending, particularly, came under attack—for several reasons. Problems of urban and environmental decay came to the fore. The mounting cost of the Viet Nam War led to cutbacks in other defense spending, including research and development. Student unrest over the war prompted several universities to cancel or refuse contracts for defense-related research.

Cutbacks in University and Industrial Research

From 1962 to 1967 there was a steady growth in annual federal support of science at the college level—from $1.6 billion to $2.5 billion. By 1969 the support had dropped to $1.2 billion. Although there has since been some increase, the amount of increase is not regarded by the colleges as enough to offset the effects of inflation. Jerome B. Wiesner has said that if this is more than a temporary interlude, it could be a threat to America's capacity to "make the transition to society-oriented scientific work"—research aimed at solving problems of the environment, cities and the like.

American business, beset by declining profits in a recession, "is turning away from research just at a time when the federal government is cutting back drastically on its support of such work in the universities," *Fortune* writer Dan Cordtz reported in January 1971. "As a consequence, a substantial number of industrial researchers worry that fundamental knowledge will not be expanded enough in the Seventies to provide a base for the applied research of the Eighties." [22]

---

[22] Dan Cordtz, "Bringing the Laboratory Down to Earth," *Fortune,* January 1971, pp. 106-107.

SOURCES OF R & D FUNDS

(millions of dollars)

Year	Total	Fed. govt.	Industry	Universities
1960	13,730	8,752	4,508	328
1961	14,552	9,264	4,749	371
1962	15,665	9,926	5,114	424
1963	17,371	11,219	5,449	485
1964	19,214	12,553	5,880	555
1965	20,439	13,033	6,539	615
1966	22,266	13,992	7,317	673
1967	23,642	14,449	8,134	753
1968	25,038	14,972	8,941	841
1969 (prel.)	26,175	14,979	9,957	895
1970 (est.)	26,850	14,650	10,910	930
1971 (est.)	27,850	14,735	11,780	960

SOURCE: National Science Foundation.

Cordtz reported that corporate spending on basic and applied research rose more than fourfold during a 15-year period, reaching an estimated $3 billion in 1970. "Few dogmas have permeated U.S. industry so quickly and thoroughly as the idea that research is indispensable," he said. "But for all the proved value of industrial research in the aggregate, many businessmen wonder what they are getting for their money." Exploratory work "looking down the road five to ten years and more has become a luxury few feel they can afford," he added.

Science magazine reported Dec. 17, 1971, that since October four of the leading industrial research laboratories in the United States had reduced their staffs or made major changes in the direction of their research. "So far, the actual fraction of scientists who will lose their jobs is small, and company spokesmen adamantly maintain that they are still in the business of basic research," the magazine reported. "But if other companies follow this trend, it could spell the decline, in large degree, of basic research in U.S. industry for a long time to come."

The four companies and their laboratories were identified as: U.S. Steel Corporation's Edgar C. Bain Laboratory for Fundamental Research in Monroeville, Pa.; RCA's David Sarnoff Research Center at Princeton, N.J.; Shell Oil Company's Emeryville (Calif.) Research Center; and Ford Motor Company's Scientific Research Center in Dearborn, Mich. Many small and medium-sized R & D firms have been hit hard by cutbacks in government funding. *Washingtonian* magazine reported in its January 1972 issue that "a trickle of new government contracts at the end of last year raised hopes that 1972 will put some hard-pressed research and development firms back on their feet." "Many companies," the magazine added, "have diversified out of aerospace pursuits, and into civilian projects in environmental controls, marine resources, health, education, and crime detection."

Hollomon and Harger contend that although industrial spending on research and development went up in the past 15 years, the impact has been limited by rising costs. High interest rates, for instance, retarded capital investment required to infuse new technology into the economy. Only the largest companies could afford to gamble on a basic research project. John Kenneth Galbraith, in his *New Industrial State* (1967), argued that there will be an inevitable concentration of technological and economic power in the largest companies in the future. Moreover, Galbraith said these companies would become ever more closely aligned with government.

Jean-Jacques Servan-Schreiber, the French author of *The American Challenge* (1968), agrees that modern technology thrives best in the context of giant corporations. And to meet the challenge of a wholesale takeover of European industry by American corporations, he has urged the creation of giant-sized European companies. But the evidence of technological concentration is not all one way. Morton Mintz and Jerry S. Cohen argue that large companies sometimes thwart the acceptance of new technologies and small firms are now making better use of technological improvements.

> The impact of imports of automobiles [they wrote]...should make it clear that American companies have no monopoly on advanced technology... The petroleum companies owe much of their success to government tax and import policies rather than to technological prowess... The American steel companies have been notorious for their failure to adopt new technologies... The aerospace companies depend almost entirely on the federal government for their sustenance....[23]

The authors conclude that "Europe would make a tragic error to accept the Servan-Schreiber thesis that giantism is the answer to American corporate penetration."

---

[23] Morton Mintz and Jerry S. Cohen, *America Inc.* (1971), pp. 350-352.

Directions for Technology in Seventies

CONGRESS IS NOW "quite properly asking how science, if it is to justify its support from public funds, can help government solve the difficult problems that science and technology have helped to produce," wrote Don K. Price, dean of the Kennedy School of Government at Harvard. [24] With the current prospect for large increases in government support of research and development, a long shopping list of science needs has developed. Science writer Victor Cohn has listed several items widely thought to be necessary in any new science policy. They include: 1) "bloc" or "formula" grants to universities to direct to projects of their choice; 2) a larger-scale program to help science students pay for their education; 3) abandonment of the idea of a research-oriented doctorate and substituting a more general "Doctor of Arts" degree for students headed for many kinds of jobs in science; 4) more federal financing of private research, especially basic or non-directed research; and 5) some steps to put unemployed and underemployed scientists back to work. [25]

For environmentalists, top priority in any new science policy must be a major effort to clean up the environment. Also, the anti-pollution movement has called for the creation of checks and balances to ensure that the application of any new technology will not further debase the land, water and air resources of the United States. Though pollution-control technology has made appreciable advances in recent years, it is not hard to find experts who deplore its present state. "Primitive" would accurately describe the state of anti-pollution technology, according to the editor of the American Chemical Society's monthly journal. "It's no secret that pollution control has traditionally drawn upon old concepts, old equipment, and the least skilled work force available," he wrote. "Pollution-control technology has evolved at a snail's pace." [26]

While the anti-pollution movement has gained more notice, some critics of American science believe it should be more concerned with aiding poor nations. They say that if science is pressed to improve productivity and increase industrial might,

---

[24] Don K. Price, "Science at a Policy Crossroads," *Technology Review*, April 1971, p. 37.

[25] Victor Cohn, "Science in the Begabuck Era," *Technology Review*, February 1971, pp. 8-9.

[26] D. H. Michael Bowen, "Build a Better Mousetrap" (editorial), *Environmental Science and Technology*, November 1970, p. 877. See also "Pollution Technology," *E.R.R.*, 1971 Vol. I, pp. 3-24.

it will only widen the economic gap between rich and poor nations. Eugene Rabinowitch, editor-in-chief of the *Bulletin of the Atomic Scientists,* has written that, important as the pollution problem is, "I am convinced that development of the underdeveloped countries is the key to the future of mankind." "This danger is real, more than the danger of technological civilization in the advanced countries sinking in the morass of pollution—although at the present time, the latter danger is much more acutely troubling the Western mind." [27]

Estimates of what it will cost to put and keep the environment in good order are imprecise and variable, but all agree that it will be enormously high. Stewart L. Udall, former Secretary of the Interior, said in 1970 that a comprehensive program to control water pollution alone would cost $30 billion in the four years ahead. Marshall I. Goldman, a professor of economics at Wellesley College, has estimated that $130 to $180 billion would be required to construct needed facilities to control both air and water pollution and $12 to $17 billion to operate them every year.

Debate Over Support For Basic or Applied Research

Emilio Q. Daddario has said that after World War II science was enshrined by the public as a 20th century value, "inviolate and, like Caesar's wife, above reproach." In addition, a "laissez-faire attitude grew up with regard to the conduct of research: scientists could study anything they wished." Today, however, "science and scientists themselves must be more responsive to the needs of the society which, through its support, makes their work possible."[28] In apparent agreement that science should be directed toward the resolution of specific problems. Alvin Toffler has written: "We need a broad political grouping rationally committed to further scientific research and technological advance—but on a selected basis only." [29]

Others see drawbacks in "mission-oriented" research. Presidential Science Adviser Edward E. David Jr. believes that it "has a tendency to be somewhat myopic." He points out that the laser was developed out of basic research in microwave spectroscopy. "There was no apparent importance of this field in terms of the missions of laboratories and agencies. Out of

[27] Eugene Rabinowitch, "The Role of Scientists: Thoughts for 1971" (editorial), *Bulletin of the Atomic Scientists,* January 1971, p. 4.

[28] Emilio Q. Daddario, "National Science Policy—Prelude to Global Cooperation," *Bulletin of the Atomic Scientists,* June 1971, p. 23.

[29] Alvin Toffler, *Future Shock* (1970), pp. 382-383.

work which was supported as basic by the government and some basic research elements of industry came the concepts behind the laser—and eventually its implementation." David concluded: "Though I sympathize with relevance in research, I think that it can be carried too far... It can be highly counter-productive and wasteful." [30]

However, Thomas O'Toole, science writer of *The Washington Post*, reported Jan. 2, 1972, that the Nixon administration was preparing to place more emphasis on research that would produce quick and practical benefits for society. "The change in science policy contemplated by the Nixon administration would be the most sweeping to hit science in 20 years—sweeping in the sense that it could alter the mix of applied and pure research done in the United States, largely at the expense of pure research," O'Toole said.

He said one of the few science programs of any size begun by the Nixon administration is a $49 million project at the National Science Foundation code-named RANN—for Research Applied to National Needs. It "supports a host of small programs aimed at improving things like subways, cancer treatment, earthquake forecasting and sewers." In addition, O'Toole reported, "the time is coming...when the space agency will be asked to drop most of its studies of planets and stars to use its manpower to develop solar cells and fuel cells (both used to power spacecraft) to provide electricity on Earth."

The space agency recently formed a new Office of Space Applications and increased its budget for "technology utilization." In the past six months it has agreed to undertake study projects for the departments of Commerce, Interior and Transportation on problems having nothing to do with space exploration. "One reliable report suggests that between $2 billion and $4 billion of federal research money will be 're-programmed' in the next fiscal 1972 budget," O'Toole said. The re-programming is seen by Washington observers as being largely in the hands of William Magruder, manager of the New Technological Opportunities Program.

Sharing of Federally Acquired Data With Businesses

Jennings Randolph (D W.Va.), chairman of the Senate Small Business Subcommittee on Science and Technology, warned in February 1970 that thousands of small subcontractors would be "swept away" if they did not adopt new

---

[30] Edward E. David Jr., "Toward New Initiatives," *Technology Review*, February 1971, p. 26.

techniques. "There is nothing more important for the small manufacturer...than to gain access to the technology data banks that can guide him in making the required adjustments." Congress has interested itself several times in improving the transfer of available technological information to industry but has always been troubled over policy questions. When research has been paid for by the taxpayers, should it be made available to business for private profit? Congress tried to resolve the issue by setting forth conditions but yet easing the transfer of such information under terms of the State Technical Services Act of 1965.

There are several technology data banks in the United States, including the Scientific and Technical Aerospace Reports, the Science Information Exchange, and Chemical Abstracts. Technology data in the public domain can be found most readily through the National Technical Information Services Branch of the Commerce Department. Richard N. Foster wrote recently that "organizations that rely on technical innovation to increase market shares will have to reap more from past, as well as present, investments in science and technology if they hope to maintain their competitive clout." [31] Foster urges companies to create "tech transfer teams" whose job it is to survey the resource base and come up with suggestions for applications of off-the-shelf technologies.

On a larger scale, however, America's lagging technological achievement is expected to be invigorated by government, not business. The idea of governmental assistance for—if not outright sponsorship of—research and development is now firmly entrenched in American society. It appears certain that expenditures on technology will increase, perhaps dramatically, under the spur of the 1971 trade deficit. What remains to be seen is how well the government and science meet the complaints of environmentalists and others—many of whom argue that what America needs is less technology, not more.

---

[31] Richard N. Foster (director of the Technology Management Group, Abt Associates, Inc.), "Organize for Technology Transfer," *Harvard Business Review*, November-December 1971.

EDUCATION FOR JOBS

by

Mary Costello

1 9 7 1
Nov. 3

EDUCATION FOR JOBS

VOCATIONAL EDUCATION—training for the world of work that does not require a bachelor's degree—has long been considered the stepchild of American education. The stepchild has emerged during the past few years to become a subject of increasing public concern. Sidney P. Marland Jr., U.S. Commissioner of Education, had good reason to call vocational training the No. 1 priority in education. A recent study by the Department of Labor indicates that by 1980 about 80 per cent of all jobs will require less than a bachelor's degree but very few will be available to the unskilled. It is estimated that over 40 million of the 46 million students now in school will not graduate from college.[1] Without some kind of vocational training, many of these young people will be unable to find work.

Even a college degree offered no assurance of a job in the year 1971 and, according to numerous forecasts, job prospects would remain dim in several professions for years to come. Professional journals and the popular press told of overcrowding in many fields and of large numbers of new graduates being left unemployed.[2] Even holders of advance degrees were not immune from these conditions. The Ph.D. was no longer a meal ticket, especially in teaching and engineering, two of the professions hardest hit by changes in the job market.[3] These changes were being wrought by such diverse factors as uncertainty in the national economy, a slippage in the rate of population growth, and a large outpouring of graduates in the past decade.[4]

---

[1] Russell Flanders, "Employment Patterns for the Seventies," *Compact* (publication of the Education Commission on the States, Denver, Colo.), August 1970, p. 7.

[2] For example, see "Let's Break the Go-to-College Lockstep," *Fortune,* November 1970, and "As Traditional Job Markets Shift, State Colleges Seek New Educational Roles," *The Chronicle of Higher Education,* Nov. 1, 1971.

[3] See "As the Surplus of Teachers Grows," *U.S. News & World Report,* Oct. 25, 1971, p. 44.

[4] "From 1861, when Yale became the first American university to grant the Ph.D., through 1970, American universities awarded 340,000 doctor's degrees. Half of these degrees were awarded in the last nine years of that period. If current projections...are borne out, another 340,000 (and probably more) will be awarded in the 1971-80 decade."—Dael Wolfle and Charles V. Kidd, "The Future Market for Ph.D.'s," *Science,* Aug. 27, 1971, p. 784.

"At a time when there is a glut of Ph.D.'s, and perhaps 65,000 engineers are out of work," *Business Week* observed, "many jobs cannot find people." "This year...only about 38 per cent of the jobs for sub-professional health workers will be filled by trained people. By 1980 the nation is expected to be short 400,000 such workers, trained or not. In the next four years, some 1.5 million more secretaries will be needed, the number of people employed in certain computer fields should double, and such comparatively new areas as pollution control will increase the need for technicians."[5]

Fading Stigma of Trade Schools Among Students

Despite the opportunities for vocationally educated students, there remains a deep prejudice in many quarters against such training. The first annual report of the National Advisory Council on Vocational Education in 1968 stated:

> At the very heart of our problem is a national attitude that says vocational education is for somebody else's children.... We [Americans] have promoted the idea that the only good education is an education capped by four years of college. This idea...is snobbish, undemocratic, and a revelation of why schools fail so many students.

Dr. Bruno Battelheim, professor of psychiatry at the University of California, told a congressional subcommittee in 1969: "In my opinion, there are today far too many students in the colleges who have no business to be there....Many would be better off in a high-level program of vocational education which is closely linked to a work program...."[6]

The stigma of vocational education is fading, though slowly, as student disillusionment with college education increases. The scarcity of jobs for graduates, especially those in the liberal arts, is encouraging many young people to forego four years of college for vocational training after they finish high school. A trend is already apparent. The nation's college enrollment in the fall of 1971, as estimated by the U.S. Office of Education, showed the smallest rate of growth (6 per cent) in a decade *(see table, page 106)*

The total number of trainees in vocational programs of all types, including those in high school, stood at 9.5 million in 1970 *(see table, opposite page)*. The U.S. Office of Education estimated that when the fall 1971 figures are finally compiled,

[5] "Blue-Collar Training Gets a White-Collar Look," *Business Week*, July 31, 1971, p. 76. See also "Jobs for the Future," *E.R.R.*, 1969 Vol. II, pp. 919-935.

[6] Testimony before the House Special Subcommittee on Education, March 20, 1969.

VOCATIONAL EDUCATION FINANCING AND ENROLLMENT

Fiscal year	Funds Expended			Enrollments			
	State and local	State, local and federal	High school	Post-high school	Adult	Special needs
	(in thousands)			(in thousands)			
1961	$206,063	$254,073		not available		
1965	447,709	604,645	2,819	207	2,379	26
1966	566,100	799,894	3,048	442	2,531	49
1967	743,812	1,004,133	3,533	500	2,941	74
1968	939,479	1,192,862	3,843	593	2,987	111
1969	1,114,080	1,368,756	4,079	706	3,050	143
1970	1,405,651	1,784,515	5,075*	997*	2,650*	769*

*New Hampshire and North Carolina figures not available; 1969 state totals substituted.
SOURCE: American Vocational Association, Washington, D.C.

they will reach 10.4 million. One expert has projected that the total will exceed 17 million in 1975.[7]

Despite the gains made by vocational education in attracting youth, it does not offer full assurance that a job lies ahead. According to statistics compiled by the U.S. Office of Education, in 1970 some 76 per cent of the high school graduates who completed vocational training and were available for jobs were able to find them in their field or related fields. The pre-1970 figure for job placement was higher—about 85 per cent. A spokesman at the Office of Education attributed the decline to general economic conditions.

Occupational Training: Its Size and Fast Growth

Vocational education at the high school level accounts for about two-thirds of all persons enrolled in job-training programs. Vocational courses may be offered in either regular or vocational-technical high schools. Educators have been debating the relative merits of the two types of high schools for years. Those favoring separate vocational-technical schools argue that these institutions are able to provide more specialized training and have better equipment and facilities. They also say that removing vocational students from the academic environment of a regular high school tends to eliminate any feeling of inferiority on their part.[8] Others argue that it is costly to maintain separate vocational schools, that

---

[7] Calvin Dellefield, "Teachers: Vocational Education's Future," *Compact*, August 1970, p. 26.

[8] In a study of vocational education in Massachusetts, published in 1968, Carl Schaeffer and Jacob Kaufman reported that one-third of the graduates of the vocational curriculum in regular high schools felt that they had been looked down upon because of choice of study.—Cited by Rupert N. Evans in *Foundations of Vocational Education* (1971), p. 174.

105

1971	8.4 million*	1966	5.9 million
1970	7.9 million	1965	5.5 million
1969	7.4 million	1964	4.9 million
1968	6.9 million	1963	4.5 million
1967	6.4 million	1962	4.2 million

*Estimate of U.S. Office of Education.

---

these schools have high dropout rates, and that they foster socio-economic segregation.

Increasing numbers of students exposed to vocational education in high school are entering community colleges. More than 1,000 community colleges are in existence, twice as many as 10 years ago. Their enrollment has more than tripled since 1960, reaching two million, a figure that is expected to double by 1980. "The community college has proved its great worth to American society," the Carnegie Commission on Higher Education said in June 1970. "Occupational programs should be given the fullest support and status within community colleges. These programs need to be flexibly geared to the changing requirements of society."[9]

One of the problems facing community colleges is the relationship between liberal arts and career curricula. A frequent criticism is that teachers are geared to academic rather than vocational instruction and are primarily interested in students who plan to transfer to four-year colleges. Vocational students are often forced to take traditional college courses in which they are not interested. Kenneth B. Holt of the University of Maryland College of Education has recommended that community colleges "eliminate the artificial requirements of liberal arts courses for those who wish vocational education." To do so, he wrote, "would immediately draw many more vocational education students to the campus and would reduce the dropout rate among those now in attendance."[10]

Dropout rates in community colleges are high; 60 to 70 per cent of all students who enter and 90 per cent of students from low-income homes drop out before completion of the two-year program. Despite these problems, Dr. Holt believes that "the community college movement itself holds great potential

[9] However, the Carnegie Commission still extolls the virtues of earning a college degree. A commission report due for publication in the fall of 1971 purports to show that college graduates are higher paid (see table, page 111) and tend to be more satisfied in their jobs than others.

[10] Kenneth B. Holt, "The Community College Must Change," Compact, August 1970, p. 37.

for combatting the prevalent biased view of vocational education."

"The student in a vocational education program must be taught skills and content relevant to the entry-level job he is aiming at," according to Lowell A. Burkett, executive-director of the American Vocational Association. "Linkage with manpower trainers are required to insure the relevance....The most effective and immediate linkage—one which can scarcely be improved—is the cooperative vocational program. Cooperative education contains elements of apprenticeship training; it is on-the-job experience coupled with related subject matter and is perhaps the best example of linkage between vocational educator and manpower trainer."[11]

Interest of Businesses in Vocational Education

Students in cooperative programs are able to apply what they have learned in the classroom to actual job conditions. And because training in these programs is closely related to full-time employment, cooperative programs are far more responsive to changes in the labor market than completely school-based programs. Examples of cooperative programs include the Chrysler-Northwestern Program and Philadelphia's Business Experience and Education Program (BEEP).

After the 1967 riots in Detroit, the Chrysler Corporation renovated a wing of the city's predominantly black Northwestern High School and established a program to train auto mechanics and a placement office where industry personnel could test and interview the trainees. In addition, teaching grants were awarded to Northwestern instructors who wanted to develop new programs. In the Philadelphia program, public schools have cooperative work-study arrangements with about 20 employers. The participating students, almost 4,000 of them, receive on-the-job training and earn money for their labors. In 1969-70, their average earnings were $960.

In addition to participating in cooperative programs, many large companies are establishing their own schools. Ross Sackett, vice-president of the Columbia Broadcasting System, contends that his organization "has a major strategic commitment to operate well-run, quality schools because public education hasn't done the job."[12] Industry schools can be extremely profitable. National Systems Corporation was

---

[11] Quoted in Roman C. Pucinski and Sharlene Hirsch (eds.), *The Courage to Change: New Directions for Career Education* (1971), p. 154.

[12] Quoted in *Business Week*, July 31, 1971, p. 76. See also "Education Market," *E.R.R.*, 1966 Vol. II, p. 927.

reported to have grossed more than $15 million in 1970 operating courses for 50,000 students. Tuition per student at Honeywell Institute of Information Sciences is $1,900 a year; at five schools operated by Radio Corporation of America it is $1,400; and for computer studies courses conducted by Bell & Howell Co. it is $1,300. Students appear willing to pay high tuition when there is a good chance they will get a job in the company when they complete the program. RCA, for example, places about 90 per cent of its graduates.

In addition to specific industry-run training schools, more than 7,000 private career schools operate in this country. These institutions enrolled about two million students in 1970 and collected about $2 billion in tuition.[13] The Federal Trade Commission held hearings in 1970 arising from complaints that certain career schools had not delivered either the training or the jobs promised in their advertisements. The FTC can take only remedial action, that of issuing "cease and desist" orders, when it finds that a complaint is valid. Only if the orders are ignored is the offender subject to a fine (up to $5,000). Some 20 states and the District of Columbia have no laws regulating these schools. The U.S. Office of Education has delegated authority for accrediting career schools to the National Association of Trade and Technical Schools; its membership is made up of the owners of trade schools.

The Washington Post published a series of stories between July 11 and 15, 1971, dealing with private career schools and the recruiting practices some of them used. Thomas Austin, a former director of a school operated in Washington by Career Enterprises, Inc., was quoted as saying: "You make real money by signing people up. The whole system is designed for everybody to put pressure on the man below him to go out and get students. In the process, everybody forgets about the students."

Academic vs. Occupational Instruction

THEORIES ABOUT THE IMPORTANCE or wastefulness of vocational education have a long history. In his *Laws*, Plato wrote that training for manual skills is "mean and illiberal, and is not worthy to be called education at all." In

---

[13] Figures reported by *The Washington Post*, July 13, 1971.

contrast, Martin Luther advised the mayors and aldermen in Germany in 1524: "Boys should spend an hour or two a day in school, and the rest of the time work at home, learn some trade and do whatever is desired so that study and work may go together, while the children are young and can attend to both."

The 18th century philosopher Jean Jacques Rousseau, in his revolt against the intellectualism in the French education system, painted a rather idyllic picture of manual training in *Emile*, published in 1762. To learn the carpentry trade, Emile spent two days a week with a master carpenter. Rousseau's book had a direct influence on the Swiss educator Johann Heinrich Pestalozzi, who organized a school embodying many of Rousseau's ideas. Pestalozzi believed that a child learns by doing. Books were to be used "to supplement experience, and to supply those facts that are not readily accessible by direct investigation."[14]

Pestalozzi's theories were brought to the United States by his pupil Francis Joseph Neff, who taught in a number of American schools before he was called to New Harmony, Ind., in 1825 to teach in a school founded by Robert Owen. Owen was in complete sympathy with the Pestalozzi method and called repeatedly for education "combining mechanical and agricultural with literary and scientific instruction...making every scholar a workman and every workman a scholar."

Gradually Owen's idea of combining general and vocational education grew and was embodied in the American land-grant colleges in the second half of the 19th century. The American educator John Dewey argued that education was a tool to help the citizen combine culture and vocation. Dewey wrote: "Our culture must be consonant with realistic science and with machine industry instead of a refuge from them. And while there is no guaranty that an education which uses science and employs the controlled processes of industry as a regular part of its equipment will succeed, there is every assurance that an educational practice which sets science and industry in opposition to its ideal of culture will fail."[15]

However, with few exceptions, the idea that vocations should be taught in the schools was unacceptable to American educators. "American educational philosophy was merely a

[14] Quoted by Melvin Barlow in *History of Industrial Education in the United States* (1967), p. 22.

[15] John Dewey, "American Education and Culture," *The New Republic*, July 1, 1916, p. 216.

modification of English educational thought: it was essentially aristocratic and not democratic in its basic philosophy. The aristocratic concept of education held that education must be designed to meet the needs of the 'gentleman class.' If any of the 'laboring class' was willing or able to acquire such education, the educator did not object; in fact, he often urged the importance, in America, of taking 'culture' to the 'laboring classes' in order that they might be 'elevated,' "[16]

The idea that a liberal arts education was the best preparation for any vocation was stressed by many American educators well into the 20th century. As late as 1944, Robert Maynard Hutchins, president of the University of Chicago, remarked: "The thing to do with vocational education is to forget it.... The task of the educational system is not to train hands for industry, but to prepare enlightened citizens for our democracy and to enrich the life of the individual by giving him a sense of purpose which will illuminate not merely the 40 hours he works but the 72 he does not."

John W. Gardner, former Secretary of Health, Education and Welfare, takes a different view. He has written: "We live in a society which honors poor philosophy because philosophy is an honorable calling, and ignores good plumbing because plumbing is a humble occupation. Under such practices, we will have neither good philosophy nor good plumbing. Neither our pipes nor our theories will hold water."[17]

Emergence of Job Training in American Schools

Vocational education in the United States developed in three stages: (1) through apprenticeship, (2) in private schools and colleges, and (3) in the public schools. The Industrial Revolution which reached America in the early 19th century severely weakened the system of domestic apprenticeship. In that system, the trainee lived with his master who taught him the trade and provided him with food and clothing. The need for skilled workers and the decline of apprenticeship led to the establishment of a number of private vocational schools.

The Gardner Lyceum, the first school devoted entirely to practical studies like surveying, navigation, farming, carpentry and civil architecture, was opened in Maine in 1823. A year later, the Rensselaer Polytechnic Institute was founded in Troy, N.Y., to "apply science to the common purposes of

---

[16] Arthur B. Mays, *Principles and Practices of Vocational Education* (1948), p. 43.

[17] John W. Gardner, *Excellence: Can We Be Equal and Excellent Too?* (1969), p. 86.

INCOME LEVELS AND EDUCATION

Education of head of family	Family mean income	Number of cases	Education of head of family	Family mean income	Number of cases
Grades 0-5	$4,000	143	Grade 12 plus non-college training	$9,890	264
Grades 6-8	6,300	410	College, no degree	10,830	329
Grades 9-11	8,820	402	Bachelor's degree	13,030	239
Grade 12	9,480	415	Advanced or professional degree	16,460	109

SOURCE: Carnegie Commission on Higher Education.

life." These and a number of other private institutions were beset by lack of cooperation from the academic community. The majority of those established before the Civil War failed.

The Morrill Act in 1862 provided grants of land to endow, support and maintain state colleges devoted to agriculture and the practical arts "to promote the liberal and practical education of the industrial classes" (see page 113). It was not until the 1880s that this concept of combining academic and vocational education was introduced into the secondary schools. A major reason for the delay was that the high schools had been used chiefly to prepare boys for college. In 1870, 80 per cent of all high school graduates went on to college. Beginning in 1880, with the adoption of compulsory school attendance laws in many states, high school enrollment doubled every 10 years while college enrollment grew more slowly.

As the high school became the terminal point in the education of many young people, public demand for practical, career-minded education grew. The result was the merger of manual and academic training in the secondary school curriculum. Manual training was not conceived of as vocational training but as an attempt to "infuse new vitality into old curricula, to rouse student interest in school programs, to promote more sensible occupational choices, to raise the educational level of the laboring classes, and to elevate all occupations to a millennium of culture and refinement."[18]

Calvin M. Woodward, dean of the Washington University polytechnic faculty, opened the first manual training high school in St. Louis in 1880. Woodward's goal was a combination of mental and manual instruction, one which would "put the whole boy in school, his hands as well as his head." In

---

[18] Grant Vern, Man, Education and Work (1964), p. 49.

111

less than four years, enrollment in Woodward's school increased from 50 to over 200. Similar schools were set up in many communities throughout the country. Other cities added manual training to their general high school programs.

However, near the turn of the century, some educators began to complain that the program of trying to train students for all vocations was actually training them for none. Many vocationalists believed that the only solution was the establishment of a separate public high school system devoted solely to vocational courses. This dual system of education was attacked by John Dewey and others as undemocratic. While the dual system in which administration and control of vocational and regular high schools are separate has not gained widespread acceptance in this country, a *de facto* dual system has emerged. State boards of vocational education, usually under the regular board of education, have become more influential. The emergence of area vocational high schools has tended to reinforce this duality.

Approaches to Career Education in Soviet Union

In the United States, vocational education seldom begins before junior high school. In the Soviet Union, it starts much earlier. A Soviet educator has written: "Our general education school is also a trade and polytechnic school. From the very first elementary grades the children are taught how to handle simple tools and do simple repairs, the kind of thing every person needs to know, no matter what trade or profession he picks later. In the high schools, general education and polytechnic training go hand in hand. The teacher in each subject not only gives her students the theoretical knowledge, but also, to some degree, shows them how to apply it."[19] At least two hours a week of manual work is required of Russian students at every grade level. Occupational information and guidance is given even in the elementary grades. Older students work in school shops or farm plots and take courses at industrial or agricultural plants.

Before the Russian Revolution in 1917, most Russian workers were trained in apprenticeship programs. In the early 1920s, factory training schools were set up to provide both general and vocational education. These ran three to four years and required from four to seven years of previous general education. By 1937, factory training schools had prepared about two million skilled workers. But because every factory trained

[19] Tamila Zhurbitskaya, "The YCL in the High School," *Soviet Life,* May 1971, p. 52.

workers to meet its own needs, it was felt that a nationwide system geared to meet the needs of the whole country was essential.

To this end, a comprehensive system of vocational and industrial training schools was established in 1940. These schools at first required from four to six years of previous schooling; now at least eight, and preferably 10, years of general education are required for admission. The course of study is usually two years for those who have completed 10 years of general education and four years for those who left after eight years. Vocational school students divide their time between classroom and work experience. From four to six months a year are spent in apprenticeship training at factories, construction sites and state farms. Tuition, food, clothing, textbooks and accommodations are provided at no cost to the student.

Urban vocational schools train students for specific crafts in industry, construction, transportation, communications and public utilities, while rural schools prepare them to be farm machine operators, tractor drivers, electricians, mechanics and builders. The Committee for Vocational Training works closely with economic planning bodies to ensure that the Russian vocational schools train students to meet new technological and manpower requirements. Almost two million students were reported to be enrolled in the Soviet Union's 4,800 vocational-technical schools in 1971.

Federal Aid Via Morrill and Smith-Hughes Acts

During the 19th century, most financial aid for American vocational education was of state and local origin. Federal money was limited to the agricultural and mechanic arts. Under the first Morrill Act of 1862, the federal government donated "public lands to the several states and territories which may provide colleges for the benefit of agriculture and the mechanic arts." Twenty-five years later, the Hatch Act provided each state $15,000 to "establish agricultural experiment stations to aid in acquiring and diffusing among the people of the United States useful and practical information respecting the principle and application of agricultural science." The second Morrill Act of 1890 provided another $15,000 annually for each of the land-grant colleges.

In the early years of the 20th century, a number of commissions were established to investigate vocational education needs and recommend programs for satisfying those needs. Invariably, these commissions advocated a great expansion of vocational education facilities at public expense. The Commission on National Aid to Vocational Education recommended to Congress in 1914 that national grants be made because the problem was too large to be worked out on a local basis. The commission's recommendations became the basis of the National Vocational Education (Smith-Hughes) Act of 1917. This act provided $7 million a year for teaching vocational skills in agriculture, home economics, trade and industry. By 1920, enrollment in federally subsidized programs had doubled and federal, state and local expenditures had quadrupled.

Congress increased federal support of vocational education in subsequent legislation. The George-Reed Act of 1929 authorized the additional spending of $1 million a year to expand agriculture and home economics programs, the George-Ellzey Act of 1934 increased the supplementary funds to $3 million, and the George-Deen Act of 1936 added $14 million to the basic $7 million Smith-Hughes grant. During World War II, Congress spent more than $100 million to finance a Vocational Education National Defense program for training seven million war-production workers. The George-Barden Act of 1946 provided $29 million for training in agriculture, home economics, trades and industry. Sen. Walter F. George (D Ga., 1922-57) was co-author of the foregoing laws.

Enlarged Federal Goals and Spending for Jobs

Soon after President Kennedy took office, he told Congress that "technological changes which have occurred in all occupations" call for a review of vocational-aid laws, "with a view toward their modernization." To that end, the President established a Panel of Consultants on Vocational Education. Its report, *Education for a Changing World of Work,* issued early in 1963, argued that vocational programs were not preparing enough students for work and that there was an urgent need for technical training after high school. The panel recommended that federal appropriations for these purposes be increased from $57 million to $400 million. The Vocational Education Act of 1963, signed into law by President Johnson on Dec. 18, increased federal funding although it fell short of the amounts recommended by the panel.

Until the 1963 act was passed, federal funds for vocational education were limited to specific fields like agriculture and home economics. After 1963, these funds could be used for training in any occupation that did not require four years of college. This training could be offered in high school or afterward. Each state was required to match federal funds on a

50-50 basis. Most states contribute far more, often three times as much as they receive from the federal government.

Congress amended the act in 1968 "to provide vocational offerings so that persons of all ages in all communities of all states would have ready access to vocational training or retraining suitable to their needs and abilities." The 1968 legislation authorized $2.8 billion in federal spending over five years and required that at least 15 per cent of a state's basic allotment be spent for students who are disadvantaged mentally, physically or culturally.

Federal funds today account for about 20 per cent of all public expenditures for vocational education. These combined expenditures in 1970 amounted to $1.8 billion *(see table, p. 105)* and represented a sevenfold increase since 1961. But they still were only a small slice of the total educational pie. Federal, state and local governments spent $59.7 billion on all types of education from kindergarten through graduate school in 1970, according to estimates of the National Center for Educational Statistics in the U.S. Office of Education.

New Directions for Career Education

WASHINGTON SPENDS almost four dollars for retraining unemployed workers for every dollar it spends on "preventive programs"—those that prepare young people for employment at the beginning of their careers.[20] Hugh Calkins, chairman of the National Advisory Council on Vocational Education, has said that "this nation will never reduce its pool of unemployed until it gives as much attention to prevention as it gives to remediation."

He cited the Woodland Job Center in Cleveland where two programs have operated side by side. "One, aimed at young adults who are already unemployed, is 100 per cent financed by federal dollars. The other, for youth not yet unemployed, but destined to be if they are not trained, is conducted with 100 per cent local dollars." Calkins estimated that the flow of untrained youth into the unemployed pool amounts to about 750,000 young persons a year. "For the federal govern-

---

[20] The federal government spent at least $1.5 billion for retraining unemployed workers in 1970, compared with spending of $376 on vocational education. For background on federal retraining programs, see Congressional Quarterly's *Congress and the Nation*, Vol. II (1969), pp. 734-743.

ment to train half this number of young people, at an estimated cost of $1,500 each, and to provide a stipend of about the same amount to each, would cost...$1,125,000,000 each year. By contrast, if improved vocational education in the nation's high schools could lure the same number of students back into the schools, and if the federal government were to pay the additional cost of the vocational education program...the cost would only be 25 per cent as high."[21]

Federal Testing of Proposals in Career Education

More than seven of every 10 junior and senior high school students were enrolled in general and academic programs in the past school year, although only two of the seven can be expected to complete four years of college.[22] U.S. Commissioner of Education Marland spoke of this problem to the National Association of Secondary School Principals in Houston, Texas, Jan. 23, 1971: "Eight out of 10 high school students should be getting occupational training of some sort. But only two of these eight students are....Consequently, half of our high school students, approximately 1,500,000 a year, are being offered what amounts to irrelevant, general education pap."

> Almost all of the shockingly high number of unemployed youths are products of the general curriculum [he continued] and we can expect small improvement until the general curriculum is completely done away with in favor of a system of high school education with but two exits—continued education or employment—and nothing else."

Marland suggested dropping the term "vocational education" in favor of "career education." "While it [career education] will necessarily and properly embrace many of vocational-technical education's skill-producing activities, it will also reach a large percentage of students now unexposed to the usual vocational education offerings. Instead of slightly less than 25 per cent of high school students now enrolled in some kind of vocational skills program, for example, the career education concept would affect, and affect in a fundamental fashion, as high as 80 per cent of these young people."

The National Center for Education Research and Development in the U.S. Office of Education has devised three plans for career education as substitutes for traditional general and vocational education. The first plan emphasizes career development from kindergarten through grade 12. As envisioned,

[21] Hugh Calkins, "Comprehensive Manpower Development Legislation: A Proposal," *Compact,* August 1970, pp. 15-16.

[22] William G. Loomis, "Career Education," *American Education,* March 1971, pp. 3-4.

MAJOR FEDERALLY SUPPORTED MANPOWER PROGRAMS

Program	Trainees	Adminis-tered by	FY 1969 approp.	FY 1970 approp.	FY 1971 approp.
Manpower Development Training	Unemployed and under-employed adults and youths	Labor Dept., HEW	$211,358,000	$255,084,000	$268,084,000
Vocational Education	State deter-mined	HEW	255,377,278	365,347,455	412,872,583
Vocational Rehabilita-tion	Physically, mentally handicapped	HEW	266,927,455	376,207,455	446,357,000
Work Incentive Program	Aid to Fami-lies with De-pendent Children recipients	Labor Dept., HEW	94,900,000	68,000,000	60,180,400
Neighbor-hood Youth Corps	Poor as well as unem-ployed youths	Labor Dept.	323,000,000	367,800,000	456,800,000
Operation Mainstream (formerly Green Thumb)	Chronically unemployed adults in rural areas	Labor Dept.	41,000,000	41,000,000	38,800,000
New Careers	Unemployed, poor youths in urban areas	Labor Dept.	18,600,000	14,300,000	18,800,000
Concentrated Employment Program	Hard-core unemployed in selected cities	Labor Dept.	114,800,000	199,000,000	177,000,000
JOBS (Job Opportuni-ties in the Business Sector)	Hard-core unemployed in 50 largest cities	Labor Dept.	152,000,000	175,000,000	200,000,000
Job Corps	Poor school dropouts	OEO	280,000,000	170,200,000	170,935,000

SOURCES: Office of Economic Opportunity, Labor Department

---

a youngster would be introduced to a broad range of job ideas in elementary school. He could then choose a specialty in junior high school and pursue it in senior high in one of three ways—through preparation for work immediately after high school, preparation for two years of further education, or preparation for four years of college.

The second plan provides for students from 13 to 18 years old to work for various employers in the community in apprentice-type arrangements. Participating students could re-enter school and receive credit for their outside work or go forward in the work program and receive credentials at least equal to those offered by the school. The third plan is designed to make career education accessible to persons who have left school. This plan would make use of cable television, audio-visual cassettes, telephone and correspondence courses.[23]

The Office of Education has awarded contracts amounting to $4.6 million to develop these plans. The Center for Research and Leadership Development in Vocational and Technical Education at Ohio State University has received $2 million on the first one. Another $2 million has been given to two educational laboratories, Research for Better Schools in Philadelphia and the Far West Laboratory in Berkeley, Calif., for feasibility studies on the second plan. In addition, the Center for Urban Education in New York City has been awarded $300,000 to study existing programs which could be used in developing this plan. The Education Development Center in Newton, Mass., has received a $300,000 grant for work on the third plan.

Innovative Work Programs Being Tried in Schools

While the federal government is experimenting, many innovative programs are being carried out on the local level. The Seattle public school system has integrated career information and experience into the curriculum from kindergarten through grade 12 since 1965. Young children are introduced to different types of workers and the roles they play in the community. A second grader might learn to bake bread in mathematics and measurements classes. Junior high students choose from 30 courses dealing with career skills. Career courses in senior high are developed only at the request and with the cooperation of local labor, industry and business people, thus ensuring that the training fits local needs.

A course in "Marine Engine Maintenance and Repair" was offered in two Seattle high schools after a survey of boat dealers in the area revealed a critical shortage of trained repair personnel. Local boat dealers provide on-the-job training for which students receive pay and school credits. Seattle public schools have also established a computerized data system to let students know what jobs are available

---

[23] See "Cable Television: The Coming Medium," *E.R.R.*, 1970 Vol. II, p. 669, and "Video Revolution: Cassettes and Recorders," *E.R.R.*, 1971 Vol. I, p. 227.

and what fields are likely to need skilled workers in the next few years.[24]

Many schools are using the cluster approach to career education. A student is taught the skills of related occupations which have similar knowledge requirements. This permits him to keep his career options open through high school and pursue advanced training in any one of several fields. Thus, changes in technology or manpower supply will not so readily render his skills obsolete. The Quincy, Mass., Vocational-Technical High School has developed 11 career programs providing instruction in more than 250 jobs. The programs are business education, computer data processing, electronics, food preparation, general piping, general woodworking, graphic and commercial arts, health occupations, home economics, metals and machines, and power mechanics.

Union High School in Hughson, Calif., has integrated vocational and academic education through a "learning management system." Students spend 20 per cent of their time being instructed in large groups, 40 per cent in small classes, and 40 per cent in individual study. No grades are given and students proceed at their own speed. Only two students have dropped out in the past two years, compared with 30 per cent of the student body before the new curriculum went into effect.

The Work Opportunity Center (Woc) of Minneapolis is one of a growing number of experimental institutions established to provide school dropouts and potential dropouts of ages 16 to 21 with marketable skills. Students may enter the program whenever they wish, attend as many classes as they choose, and move through the program at their own pace. High school credit is given for completion of the program. Since it was begun in 1966, over 3,000 young people have graduated from Woc. Instruction is provided in electronics and electricity, engine repair, machine work, office skills, home economics, health care, marketing and merchandising, food service, and auto mechanics.

These programs and many others like them give some indication of how far vocational or career education has come in the past decade. The stereotype vocational program held in dingy high school basements, where the least talented and disciplined students endlessly hammer pieces of wood together until they are allowed to leave school, bears little resem-

---

[24] See Vivian Hedrich, "Seattle's Concentration on Careers," *American Education*, July 1971, pp. 12-15.

blance to contemporary programs. There are still problems, to be sure. These include widespread public prejudice against vocational training, ignorance of its aims and innovations and inadequate financial assistance. But as America's trillion-dollar economy comes to demand more skilled paraprofessionals, the popularity and support of vocational education are bound to increase.

UNEMPLOYMENT IN RECESSIONS

by

Ralph C. Deans

1 9 7 0
Dec. 16

UNEMPLOYMENT IN RECESSIONS

UNEMPLOYMENT OVERTOOK INFLATION as the most serious domestic issue facing the Nixon administration as 1970 drew to a close. Economic observers noted a basic shift in policy in a speech the President delivered to the National Association of Manufacturers in New York on Dec. 4. While not abandoning the battle against inflation, Nixon's emphasis was on measures to stimulate the economy enough to roll back unemployment—then standing at the highest level in more than seven years. During November, 4.8 million Americans were out of work, about two million more than a year earlier. One worker in 17 was out of a job, compared with one in 30 when Nixon came into office in 1969.

Furthermore, the *quality* of unemployment in 1970 was disturbingly different from that experienced in four previous recessions since World War II. For the first time, large numbers of white-collar workers, highly skilled technicians, and even managers and scientists were being thrown out of work. And despite month-over-month increases in the unemployment rate, inflation was persisting. Arthur F. Burns, chairman of the Federal Reserve Board, raised the question in a speech at Pepperdine College in Los Angeles on the same night Nixon was speaking in New York. Burns said it was important for the country to understand that "we are dealing, practically speaking, with a new problem—namely, persistent inflation in the face of substantial unemployment—and that the classical remedies may not work well enough."

As most analysts saw it, the rising tide of joblessness had forced a change in Nixon's "game plan" for the economy. This term, appropriated from football, was used to describe a classical program of economic restraint involving (1) stringent control over expenditures, (2) maintenance of tax revenues and (3) a restrictive monetary policy. These actions, taken at the outset of Nixon's administration, were designed to moderate the rise in prices and permit the return to a more stable rate of growth by mid-1972.

At a news conference on Dec. 10, Nixon spoke of a "second half" of the game plan in which he would adjust fiscal and monetary policies to ease unemployment. He also noted that unemployment during 1970 would average 4.9 per cent for the year, lower than the rates achieved "in any peacetime year in the Sixties." "I want to say I'm not satisfied that that is as good as we can do," the President added. "I believe that we can have a lower rate of unemployment than 5 per cent without war...that is our goal. I think we can achieve it."

According to knowledgeable observers, the increase in unemployment induced by the administration's anti-inflationary program was more than the administration bargained for. One expression of concern in Congress was the recent passage of an omnibus job-training bill to expand manpower programs over the next three years at an estimated cost of $9.5 billion. By early 1970 recession had replaced nine uninterrupted years of economic growth. And many economists considered it a casualty of the fight against inflation, which had marred prosperity since 1965 when the American military buildup began in Viet Nam.

As a rough rule of thumb, a recession is a period when the nation's gross national product in "real" terms—eliminating the effects of inflation—declines in two or more consecutive quarters. Such declines occurred in the last three months of 1969 and the first three of 1970. Recovery has been slight. However, many citizens tend to define a recession in a very personal way—whether or not they or their neighbors are out of work with little prospect of finding another job. Unemployment rose throughout 1970, as shown below in the monthly rates complied by the Bureau of Labor Statistics:

Jan. 3.9	April 4.8	July 4.7	Oct. 5.6
Feb. 4.2	May 5.0	Aug. 5.1	Nov. 5.8
March 4.4	June 4.7	Sept. 5.5	Dec.—

In a nationally televised speech on June 17, 1970, President Nixon rededicated his administration to restraining the economy "firmly and steadily." He described his program as "a little like bringing a boat into a dock." "You turn down the power well before you get to the dock and let the boat coast in." This was widely interpreted to mean that the administration would do nothing to stimulate the economy and was prepared to accept the higher level of unemployment that this policy might entail. But on July 20, Nixon told a news conference he expected the economy to be moving upward during fiscal 1972 and said it was the administration's goal to achieve

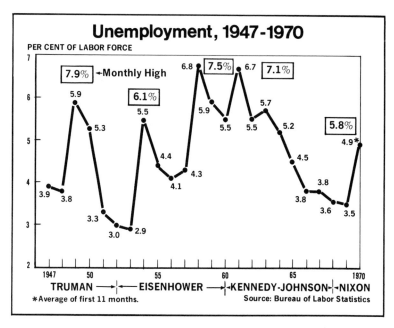

Unemployment, 1947-1970

PER CENT OF LABOR FORCE

7.9% ←Monthly High

6.1%

7.5%

7.1%

5.8%

6.8

6.7

5.9

5.9

5.5

5.7

5.7

5.5

5.5

5.2

5.3

4.9*

4.4

4.5

4.3

4.1

3.9

3.8

3.8

3.8

3.8

3.3

3.6

3.5

3.0

2.9

1947   50   55   60   65   1970

TRUMAN ──→|←── EISENHOWER ──→|←KENNEDY-JOHNSON-|←NIXON

*Average of first 11 months.   Source: Bureau of Labor Statistics

a "full employment economy" by that time. This policy was still intact when the country went to the polls in November.

Worker Layoffs as Factor in November Election

According to an election analysis by *Congressional Quarterly*, "unemployment may be assumed to have been a major factor in the Democratic gain of five House seats and the defeat of one Republican senator."[1] Unemployment would have had a wider effect on the elections but for the fact that it "was largely concentrated in major labor areas, many of which were already represented by entrenched Democrats." As a political issue, unemployment has usually benefitted Democrats since the days of Herbert Hoover, a Republican President who—rightly or not—drew the nation's blame for its worst depression in history.

Some analysts believed the unemployment issue was more important than was immediately visible on the basis of the election results. A survey of 47 districts with heavy unemployment across the country showed that in two out of three cases, the Democratic share of the vote rose significantly above the 1968 level, though often not by enough to unseat a Republican incumbent.

[1] CQ *Weekly Report*, Nov. 6, 1970, p. 2766.

Before election, the most recent figures on unemployment then available concerned the month of September, when the jobless rate was 5.5 per cent. Administration spokesmen and some independent economists regarded that high a rate as a "fluke." Harold Goldstein, Assistant Commissioner of Labor Statistics, told reporters that the unemployment survey[2] was conducted earlier than usual and may not have fully reflected the usual exit of youths from the labor market to begin the fall school term. Paul W. McCracken, chairman of the President's Council of Economic Advisers, took the unusual step of calling a news conference to tell reporters that there was no evidence of a "major deterioration in the economy" in the September statistics.

However, the unemployment rate for October, released the day after the election, showed that unemployment edged up one-tenth of a percentage point to 5.6 per cent of the labor force—the highest level since November 1963. Goldstein said it was impossible to determine whether October's 5.6 per cent unemployment "validated" the September figures.[3] Some economists argued that the October figure was also distorted by the effects of a strike at General Motors plants. Then came the November figure of 5.8 per cent, the highest since May 1963. Again it was argued that the figure was distorted, this time by the "secondary effects" of the strike.

Despite possible distortions, unemployment was high and appeared to be growing. It held definite political dangers for the Nixon administration. As the year drew to a close it was argued that joblessness must be reduced, even at the cost of more inflation—or conversely that rising inflation[4] must be stopped, even at the risk of higher unemployment. There was no agreement among economists or political commentators on which was the lesser evil or how to tackle both at once. Dr. Pierre Rinfret, a New York-based economic consultant, told President Nixon in a letter on Oct. 30, 1970, that unemployment could mount to nearly 10 per cent of the labor force in 1972—a presidential election year—if the game plan for fighting inflation was continued. However, in the wake

---

[2] The Department of Labor estimates unemployment through a monthly survey of about 52,500 households—roughly one household in every 1,170—in 449 areas throughout the country.

[3] The unemployment rate is said to be statistically "significant" at 0.2 per cent, meaning that a change of 0.2 per cent is larger than the probable error of the sample.

[4] The Consumer Price Index in October 1970 was 4.6 per cent higher than at the beginning of the year and 11.1 per cent higher than the beginning of the previous year. It had risen 24.7 per cent since July 1965, when the current wave of inflation began to appear.

of Nixon's speech on Dec. 4 Rinfret said he did not expect unemployment to exceed 6 per cent.[5] Whether or not Nixon's speech had its origin in the election returns, it signaled a turning point in the game plan.

Rise of Unemployment in White-Collar Groups

A disquieting feature of employment statistics in 1970 was a slackening in the demand for highly skilled and white-collar workers. The jobless rate for white-collar employees, which is generally impervious to a general rise in unemployment, rose significantly during the first nine months of this year. *(See table, page 128.)* "White collars are where administrators look to save money, for places to fire," noted William Gomberg, a professor at the University of Pennsylvania's Wharton School of Finance. "It's the law of supply and demand. Once you're in big supply, you're a bum."[6]

Administrators themselves were not immune. Unemployment reached deep into their ranks. "Statistics on executive unemployment are hard to come by but it is very likely that in the fall of 1970 there are more high-class, high-salaried people out of work than there have been at any time in the United States since, well, try the Great Depression of the 1930s," Bernard McCormick wrote in the magazine *Philadelphia* in October 1970. *Fortune* magazine reported the previous month that executive unemployment, "according to estimates by job recruiters and other authorities," had climbed "perhaps as high as 10 or 14 per cent."

Nor has the job market spared academia. For the first time at least since the beginning of World War II, a Ph.D. degree did not assure its holder a job—a condition that is attributed to cost-cutting by many financially hard-pressed schools and to a great outpouring of graduate students in recent years who, at least temporarily, have saturated the market. A survey of English and foreign language departments in American colleges and universities indicated the extent of belt-tightening on the campuses. The departments reported a 23 per cent decline in available new teaching positions in English between the fall of 1969 and the fall of 1970 and a corresponding decline of 27 per cent in modern foreign languages.[7]

---

[5] Interview on WTOP-TV, Washington, D.C., Dec. 4, 1970.

[6] Quoted by Judson Gooding, "The Fraying White Collar," *Fortune*, December 1970, p. 78.

[7] Survey conducted by Modern Language Association, reported in *MLA Newsletter*, November 1970, p. 1.

RATE OF WHITE COLLAR* UNEMPLOYMENT, 1970

Jan.	2.1%	April	2.9%	July	3.1%	Oct.	—
Feb.	2.3	May	2.8	Aug.	2.7	Nov.	—
March	2.7	June	2.6	Sept.	2.8	Dec.	—

* Includes professional and managerial, clerical workers and sales workers.

SOURCE: Bureau of Labor Statistics.

In the nation's public schools, the teacher shortage of years past had changed to a teacher surplus. "If you wonder how bad it is, we have a Ph.D. applying to teach third grade," said the superintendent of schools in Scarsdale, N.Y.[8] The teacher surplus stemmed primarily from the fact that the "baby boom" children who filled the classrooms in the 1950s and 1960s have finished their educations—and are entering the labor market.

Job losses among highly skilled persons in engineering and science can often be traced to federal cutbacks in defense and space programs. Seattle, Wash., and Southern California, where much of the U.S. aerospace industry is concentrated, have been particularly hard hit. And so has a semicircular corridor around Boston, its famous Route 128 along which electronics and research firms—"think tanks"—are clustered in proximity to Harvard and Massachusetts Institute of Technology. "An estimated 20,000 to 30,000 engineers are out of work in California," *U.S. News & World Report* said in a nationwide survey of unemployment it published Nov. 16, 1970. "In some areas of the country, where specialized industries have been hard hit, people with the highest skills and biggest salaries are being fired almost as fast as the least-skilled workers.

Uneven Spread of Unemployment Over Nation

Dr. Wallace Brode, former president of the American Chemical Society, estimated that 45,000 scientists and engineers were unemployed and even more were underemployed.[9] This condition was unimaginable only a few years ago. Amid Russia's spectacular space successes in the late 1950s and early 1960s, the United States considered scientists and engineers to be in desperately short supply and the government offered incentives to train tens of thousands more.

Joblessness among scientists, teachers, technicians and executives is a new and disturbing factor in today's unem-

---

[8] Quoted in *Business Week,* Aug. 22, 1970.

128

ployment figures. But the bedrock problems of unemployment among nonwhite sectors of the labor force, long-term or"chronic" unemployment, and high unemployment in specific areas continue to be the most intractable facing federal and state governments.

Unemployment rates for Negroes have consistently run almost twice as high as for whites in recent years. This disparity is laid to discrimination and a lack of education and vocational training among Negroes. Various federal programs designed to root out discrimination and to upgrade the skills of nonwhites have, so far, had only partial success, as is shown in the following table of unemployment of men over age 20, a group which comprises a majority of family breadwinners:

	Whites		Negroes and others	
	Number	Rate	Number	Rate
1968	814,000	2.0%	179,000	3.9%
1969	794,000	1.9	169,000	3.7
1970	1,517,000	3.6	293,000	6.1

Negro men are likely to experience a disproportionate share of unemployment the longer the recession continues. Ewan Clague, a former Commissioner of Labor Statistics, wrote in 1969:

> The industries which have participated most in the business expansion of the last three years will be the most vulnerable. The construction industry, housing as well as industrial-commercial, is highly susceptible to cyclical influences and particularly to high interest rates. Durable goods manufacturing is also markedly affected by a business downturn. Secondary effects will be felt in transportation and in mining.
>
> It is in these heavy industries that Negro men will experience some increases in unemployment, since they tend to have been the most recently hired employees in many instances.[9]

Paul M. Schwab, an economic analyst in the Bureau of Labor Statistics, has shown that, at least in 1968, unemployment was higher in the West than it was throughout the nation generally. An even more troublesome statistic was that nonwhite unemployment was highest in the North Central division, the upper mid-West, an area with the least amount of over-all unemployment.[10]

---

[9] Ewan Clague, *Unemployment Past, Present, and Future* (1969), published by the American Enterprise Institute for Public Policy Research.

[10] Paul M. Schwab, "Unemployment by Region and in 10 Largest States," *Monthly Labor Review*, January 1970, pp. 3-12.

The Department of Labor in the fall of 1970 listed 37 major cities and 574 smaller areas where unemployment is "substantial"—6 per cent or more of the labor force. (See page 949.) It reported that unemployment was rising more rapidly in big-city poverty areas than in the nation as a whole. In September, joblessness was recorded 46 per cent higher in poor neighborhoods of the 100 largest metropolitan areas than a year earlier. This rate outstripped a 41 per cent increase for the entire country and reversed a trend. Until September, unemployment over the nation had risen faster than in the ghettos because the impact of the business slowdown was confined largely to specialized manufacturing industries which employed few poor, unskilled workers.

Recurrent Joblessness and Federal Action

UNEMPLOYMENT, A RECURRENT PROBLEM in the United States, reached its zenith during the Great Depression of the 1930s.[11] The depression, though it lasted for 10 years after the stock market crash of Oct. 24, 1929, is generally assumed to have reached its low point in July 1932.[12] In that month, wages were 60 per cent of the 1929 level, industry was operating at half the volume of 1929 and average monthly unemployment was running at 12 million, more than a quarter of the labor force. President Hoover concentrated his efforts on aid to business through the Reconstruction Finance Corporation,[13] resisting all appeals for direct federal aid for the unemployed. While this measure was hopelessly inadequate, *Fortune* magazine, in its September 1932 issue, described it as the beginning of a new chapter in American unemployment relief. "It constitutes an open and legible acknowledgment of governmental responsibility for the welfare of the victims of industrial unemployment."[14]

---

[11] From 1879 to 1926 unemployment averaged an estimated 10.2 per cent of all workers in the manufacturing, mining and transportation fields. Even in the prosperous year of 1920, unemployment was estimated at 6.1 per cent of the labor force. See "The Extent of Unemployment," *E.R.R.*, 1930 Vol. III, p. 651.

[12] There is disagreement in academic circles to this day whether the crash caused the depression or merely preceded it. See "Wall Street: 40 Years After the Crash," *E.R.R.*, 1969 Vol. II, p. 767.

[13] Established Jan. 22, 1932, and broadened under the Emergency Relief Act approved on July 21, 1932, RFC was designed to provide capital for business expansion.

[14] Article reprinted in part in "The Great Depression," *The Annals of America,* Vol. 15 (1968), p. 167.

MAJOR AREAS OF UNEMPLOYMENT*

California
Anaheim area
Fresno
Los Angeles-Long Beach
San Bernardino area
San Diego
San Jose
Stockton

Connecticut
Bridgeport
New Britain
Waterbury

Indiana
South Bend

Kansas
Wichita

Louisiana
Baton Rouge
New Orleans

Massachusetts
Brockton
Fall River
Lawrence area
Lowell
New Bedford
Springfield-
Holyoke

Michigan
Battle Creek
Detroit
Flint
Grand Rapids
Muskegon
Saginaw

New Jersey
Jersey City
New Brunswick-
Perth Amboy

New Mexico
Albuquerque

Oregon
Portland

Texas
Corpus Christi

Washington
Seattle
Spokane
Tacoma

West Virginia
Huntington-Ashland

Wisconsin
Racine

* 6 per cent or more
SOURCE: Department of Labor

Expression of this responsibility, however, awaited the New Deal policies of President Franklin D. Roosevelt. Five days after he was inaugurated on March 4, 1933, Roosevelt convened Congress in a special session to deal with a financial crisis. He kept the legislators at work through to June 16 to pass measures to ease the plight of farmers and the unemployed. In those "Hundred Days" a wide program of social and economic experiments was enacted.

Those measures included creation of the Civilian Conservation Corps to employ young men, the Federal Emergency Relief Administration to contribute federal funds to state relief agencies, the U.S. Employment Service, and the Public Works Administration. Congress later established the Works Progress Administration to employ workers on public projects and a federal-state system of unemployment insurance. Measures such as these were credited with alleviating unemployment but they did not come close to eliminating it. In 1939, after 10 years of depression and stagnation, 9.5 million Americans, representing more than 17 per cent of the work force, were still out of work. Prosperity returned only with the coming of World War II.

Current levels of unemployment, far below those of the Thirties, approximate those experienced in four postwar recessions. (See chart, page 943.) All four were preceded by declines in business inventories, new orders for durable goods and average work week, and accompanied by falling industrial production and rising unemployment.

Unemployment During Four Postwar Recessions

As population and output rose after World War II, so did the size of the work force and the number of persons employed. But unemployment also increased relative to the labor force after each recession. The rate was substantially higher, in recovery as well as recession, in chronically depressed areas like the mill towns of New England and the coal regions of Appalachia.

The first postwar recession, in 1948-49, turned out to be relatively mild. Employment recovered in the final months of 1949 but, because of growth in the labor force, did not reach its peak until January 1950, after which it fell off rapidly. President Truman asked Congress for extension of rent controls, improved Social Security and unemployment compensation benefits. Congress approved higher minimum wages and a program of loans to states for planning public works but did not act on the remainder of Truman's proposals.

Recovery from the 1948-49 recession was well under way when the Korean War (1950-53) triggered a new boom. A slump, albeit a mild one, followed the boom at the war's end and continued into 1954. President Eisenhower, reflecting a traditional Republican "hands off" attitude, told Congress in his first Economic Report, in January 1954, that vigilance over the economy did not "justify constant stirring or meddling." Business grew better that year but not all Americans shared in the recovery. Two groups in particular were left behind: those in low-income rural areas and those in industrial areas depressed by unemployment in coal mines textile mills and other industries hit hard by technological changes.

Democrats—a number of whom had won election in 1954 on the depressed-area issue—began to press for large-scale attack on chronic unemployment. Responding to this pressure, Eisenhower said in his State of the Union message Jan. 5, 1956: "We must deal with the pockets of chronic unemployment that here and there mar the nation's general industrial prosperity." He proposed an Area Assistance Administration to loan money to needy industrial areas, but Congress refused to enact legislation to create it.

The economic expansion that began in 1954 came to an end in 1957. Business remained static through the first half of the year and then plummeted. Unlike the 1953-54 downturn, which came at a time of general price stability and declining federal expenditures, the 1957-58 recession coincided with rising prices and rising defense spending. Unemployment grew from 2.5 million in October to 5.2 million in March and then began to subside only slowly and stubbonly.

Job Creation as Goal of JFK's 'New Economics'

Traces of the third recession were still visible when the fourth began in May 1960. It was in this setting that John F. Kennedy campaigned for President on the promise of getting America "moving again." In December 1960, a month after his election, unemployment had advanced to 4.9 million, 6.8 per cent of the labor force. But the recession "bottomed out" by the following February and economic recovery proceeded steadily under the stimulus of expansionary policies that later, under the label of "New Economics," included planned budget deficits.

As in 1953, the change of administration in Washington in 1961 was accompanied by a shift in fiscal policy. Eisenhower cut the budget he inherited from Truman by $4.5 billion whereas Kennedy, upon taking office, added $8 billion to the final Eisenhower budget. Kennedy was unable to win from Congress that year a series of tax revisions to stimulate the economy—these would not be forthcoming until 1962 and 1964[15]—but he did obtain some relief for unemployed workers. Jobless benefits which normally expire after 26 weeks were prolonged an additional 13 weeks by an expedient the Eisenhower administration had used in 1958 in a similar situation. Kennedy obtained authority to advance about $1 billion to the states—which administer the benefits—to be repaid in higher federal taxes in later years.

Kennedy also asked for and received from Congress a temporary change in the federal program of matching state grants for aid to dependent children. The change enabled parents who were out of work to receive the same aid given

---

[15] See Congressional Quarterly's *Congress and the Nation*, Vol. I (1965), pp. 427-442.

to children deprived of support by reason of death, desertion or disability. Other measures increased Social Security benefits.

Still another program to reduce unemployment was the Area Redevelopment Act, twice vetoed by Eisenhower but signed into law by Kennedy on May 1, 1961. The act defined redevelopment areas in terms of high unemployment[16] and provided for the training of unemployed workers in those areas to upgrade their job skills. Congress had declared in the Employment Act of 1946 that it was a matter of national policy to "use all practicable means to promote maximum employment." But it was the Manpower Development and Training Act of 1962, to retrain workers with obsolete skills for new jobs, that put the government directly into the job-training field in a big way.

Job-training programs in the 1960s soon began to focus on youths and Negroes. Their unemployment rates were far higher than the national average, as attested by the following figures for the year 1965:

Total unemployment...	4%	Whites of ages 25-34	2.6%
Non-white youths........	20	Non-whites of ages 25-34..6.2	

The American Enterprise Institute noted that the civil rights movement, with its demands for employment opportunities for Negroes, had as much to do with the development of manpower programs in the 1960s as "the high level of unemployment carried over from the 1950s."[17]

Work-Training Programs of the War on Poverty

In its War on Poverty, the Johnson administration added the Youth Corps and the Job Corps to a cluster of job-training programs. The Youth Corps consisted of young men and women of ages 16 through 21 who were recruited from low-income families to receive work experience in federally assisted local projects. While developing job skills, and receiving pay for their work, they could continue or resume their education.

---

[16] Areas where past average annual employment had been 6 per cent or more and at least 50 per cent above the national average for three of the preceding four years; or at least 75 per cent higher for two of the preceding three years; or at least twice as high during one of the preceding two years.

[17] American Enterprise Institute for Public Policy Research, *Manpower Training and Employment Proposals*, Oct. 13, 1970, pp. 1-2. The National Advisory Commission on Civil Disorders (the Kerner Commission) estimated in its report to President Johnson in 1968 that 20 per cent of those who took part in a wave of urban riots during the preceding year were without jobs.

MAJOR FEDERALLY SUPPORTED MANPOWER PROGRAMS

Program	Trainees	Fiscal 1970 Approp.	Positions Provided
Manpower Development Training (MDTA —on-the-job training, institutional training)	Unemployed and under-employed adults and youths	$671,700,000	194,035
Vocational Education	State determined	$376,207,455	8,543,000 (enrollees)
Vocational Rehabilitation	Physically, mentally handicapped	$436,000,000	265,000 (rehabilitated)
Neighborhood Youth Corps	Poor as well as unemployed youths	$281,682,190	434,632
Operation Mainstream (formerly Green Thumb)	Chronically unemployed adults in rural areas	$ 52,043,393	17,768
New Careers	Unemployed, poor youths in urban areas	$ 15,171,563	3,846
Concentrated Employment Program (CEP)	Hard-core unemployed in selected cities	$ 49,600,000	39,000
JOBS (Job Opportunities in the Business Sector)	Hard-core unemployed in 50 largest cities	$182,600,000	107,700
Special Impact	Adult and youth slum residents in JOBS cities	$ 10,000,000 1969-70	3,500 1969-70
Job Corps	Poor school dropouts	$170,200,000	21,700

SOURCE: Manpower Report of the President (1970), pp. 193-197.

The Job Corps enrolled youths of the same ages but it differed in that work training took place in rural camps or urban training centers away from the youngsters' homes. The Job Corps soon became a focal point of opposition to anti-poverty spending; congressional foes contended that Job Corps training was costlier than a Harvard education. Like other anti-poverty programs, the Job Corps suffered budget cuts imposed by the cost of fighting a war in Viet Nam but it survived (see list above) and will be infused with new funds if an omnibus job-training bill passed by Congress late in 1970 is signed into law by President Nixon.

In its final form, as agreed to by House and Senate conferees Dec. 8, the bill would expand manpower programs during the next three years at an estimated cost of $9.5 billion. Some $200 million would be made available immediately to create a new program of public service employment. Those being trained would be placed in vacant jobs in federal, state and local governments in such fields as health, education, transportation, public safety and environmental protection.

Outlook for Achieving Full Employment

A TRADEOFF between inflation and unemployment appears to be in prospect for the immediate future. While President Nixon has promised steps to stimulate the economy, he has not abandoned the fight against inflation. In his speech to the National Association of Manufacturers on Dec. 4, 1970, the President said the federal budget he sends to Congress in the new year[18] will help promote economic growth. But he added: "If business and labor expect public policy to help stimulate real expansion then business and labor should be prepared to offer the public some real help in curing inflation."

The course of unemployment during 1971 will depend largely on how big the shift from restraint to growth will be. Some of Nixon's most influential advisers advocate an expansion of the economy rapid enough to reach 8 per cent in the last quarter of 1971, Edwin L. Dale Jr. of *The New York Times* wrote Dec. 2, 1970. That level of expansion is double the economic growth in a normally prosperous year and is seldom achieved. It would require a significant loosening of money and credit by the Federal Reserve, an agency independent of the President in theory and often in practice.

The "Fed" edged forward in that direction late in 1970 when it lowered the discount rate to ease the cost of borrowing. Changes in the discount rate, perhaps the best known economic level available to the Fed, often signal a shift in monetary policy. Twice in one month, November, the discount rate dropped by one-quarter of a percentage point—from 6 per cent where the rate had rested since April 1969 down to 5.5 per cent. The discount rate determines the rate of interest that commercial banks pay when they borrow from Federal Reserve Banks. A lowering of the discount rate is almost always followed by a lowering of the prime rate, the rate of interest commercial banks charge their best customers.[19]

Easier credit could stimulate the housing market and some other areas of the economy. An expansion of the money supply

---

[18] The President is required by law to send an annual budget to Congress within 15 days of the opening of each regular session.

[19] See "Money Supply in Inflation," *E.R.R.*, 1969 Vol. I, pp. 154-155.

usually goes hand-in-hand with an easing of credit. The Fed uses the purchase of government securities as its chief means of expanding the money supply. Large purchases are usually required to finance federal budget deficits. The prospect of a big deficit in the current fiscal year would seem to indicate the necessity of (1) a greater expansion of money supply or (2) higher taxation to reduce the approaching budget deficit. Heavier taxation, according to classical economic theory, creates unemployment rather than reduces it.

State and local governments are under considerable taxpayer pressure to scale down spending plans. Gov. Nelson A. Rockefeller ordered a series of economy measures in New York state government, including a suspension of hiring, in an effort to reduce the state budget by $100 million before the fiscal year ends on March 31, 1971. Several other states have ordered similar cutbacks. Each cutback has the effect of reducing employment.

A Gallup poll taken during October 1970 indicated that 51 per cent of the public expected unemployment to go higher during the following six months. Twenty-four per cent of those surveyed expected unemployment to remain unchanged and only 18 per cent believed fewer persons would be out of jobs. Many economists share the majority feeling that unemployment rates will increase. Dr. Charles C. Killingsworth, a professor of economics at Michigan State University and a leading manpower specialist, made the following statement in March 1970 at hearings before the Senate Labor and Welfare Subcommittee on Employment, Manpower and Poverty:

> I would say that it is likely that the national unemployment rate ...would be in excess of 5 per cent by the end of 1970; and by mid-1971, the optimistic assumption would be an unemployment rate around 6 per cent. The more pessimistic assumption is that we are now in the first stages of a recession which will go through the normal pattern; if so, we should expect an unemployment rate of 7 to 8 per cent by the middle of 1971.

Behind the development of the many manpower training programs during the early 1960s was a widespread concern that technological innovation and automation would inevitably lead to greater and greater unemployment in the face of a growing labor force. The National Commission on Technology, Automation and Economic Progress—established in 1964 to study a broad range of problems relating to unemployment— did not hold with this argument, however. In a report issued Feb. 2, 1966, the Commission concluded that it was the failure of the economy to expand rapidly enough, not automation, that was the main threat to high levels of employment. But with rising unemployment, automation is again becoming an issue today.

Underlying Causes of Current Unemployment

A substantial fraction of U.S. unemployment every year is the result of seasonal fluctuations in industry and agriculture. The Bureau of Labor Statistics estimated that early in the last decade about 20 per cent of any one year's unemployment could be attributed to seasonality.[20] The peak in over-all unemployment is not in mid-winter but in June when students looking for summer jobs flood the labor market. Construction workers regularly add to unemployment rates during the winter months, however, due to the seasonal slowdown of construction activity. While construction workers constitute only about 5 per cent of total non-agricultural employees, they account for 16 to 20 per cent of the insured unemployed persons in any given year. The Bureau of Labor Statistics eliminates these "normal" fluctuations in its monthly unemployment rates so that they represent changing economic conditions, rather than seasonal changes.[21]

There is some complaint that the unemployment figures are not accurate because they do not reflect the hard-core unemployed who, discouraged at the prospect of ever finding a job, have stopped looking for work. Similarly, the unemployment rate does not reflect the ill, disabled and handicapped who want work but are unable to obtain it.

The relationship between wage increases and unemployment was demonstrated by the British economist A. W. Phillips in a 1958 study. He found that annual wage-rate changes moved upward when unemployment was low or declining, but not when unemployment was high. This well-known "Phillips curve" is behind the theory that high rates of unemployment will eventually cure inflationary pressures created by wage demands.[22] However, some economists argue that wages and prices often bear little relation to the law of supply

---

[20] Robert J. Myers and Sol Swerdloff, "Seasonality and Construction," *Monthly Labor Review,* September 1967.

[21] "Seasonal adjustment" is a statistical technique based on the observed performance of employment and unemployment over the preceding seven calendar years. See the BLS publication, *How the Government Measures Unemployment* (1967), pp. 11-12.

[22] "The Relation Between Unemployment and the Rate of Change in Money Wage Rates in the United Kingdom, 1861-1957," *Economica,* November 1958.

and demand—that they result from the ability of powerful labor unions to raise wages or of monopolistic business enterprises to raise prices—and hence nullify the validity of the Phillips curve.

In his speech on June 17, 1970, President Nixon attributed increased unemployment and other economic ills to the transition "from a wartime economy to a peacetime economy." He noted that over 400,000 military and civilian employees had been released from the armed forces and that cutbacks in defense spending had reduced jobs by about 300,000. "While many of these workers have found new jobs, it is not hard to see where much of the current increase in total unemployment has come from," Nixon said. Unemployment was 5 per cent of the labor force when Nixon spoke.

Despite the general economic slowdown during 1969, unemployment did not begin to rise until the beginning of 1970. "Many businesses were hesitant to reduce their work forces until the slump in business proved to be more than temporary," *The Magazine of Wall Street* observed. "Moreover, because labor, especially skilled labor, had been so scarce during the recent boom, businesses did not want to lose workers in which they had invested heavily to hire and train."[23] Economists say the reverse is also true: unemployment is slow to decline in times of recovery because employers wait until they are certain business has begun to improve before they start hiring.

W. Willard Wirtz, who struggled with manpower problems as Secretary of Labor under Presidents Kennedy and Johnson, believes the root cause of unemployment is overpopulation. "It became obvious to me several years ago that there are too few jobs because there are too many people."[24] Wirtz is chairman of the National Congress on Optimum Population and Environment, a group dedicated to mobilizing population control efforts.

His concern was emphasized in the Labor Department's decennial study of U.S. manpower, released by the present Secretary of Labor, James D. Hodgson, on Nov. 10, 1970. The study forecast an increase of 15 million in the labor force during the 1970s, lifting it to a total of 100 million by 1980. While the greatest growth will occur in the age group 25-34

---

[23] "Economic Growth, Inflation and Employment," *The Magazine of Wall Street*, Oct. 25, 1970, pp. 9-11.

[24] Quoted in *The Christian Science Monitor*, May 23, 1970.

LABOR FORCE, BY AGES

Age Group	Per Cent Change 1960-1970	Per Cent Change 1970-1980	Age Group	Per Cent Change 1960-1970	Per Cent Change 1970-1980
16-24	53	19	45-54	15	- 4
25-34	16	49	55-64	21	14
35-44	- 1	13	65 and over	- 8	6
			Total labor force	18	18.3

(see table above), Hodgson said blacks will enter the work force at a rate nearly five times faster than whites.

According to the manpower study, there will be 37 million women workers by 1980, compared with 30 million in 1969 and 18 million in 1950. This increase represented "a major change in American life style," it said. "Opportunity for women to enter the professions must be improved and many employers will adjust work schedules to permit the utilization of the skills of those women able to work only on a part-time basis."[25] Throughout the 1970s, the study calculated, there will be a continuation of the shift from blue-collar to white-collar jobs, although it estimated there will be 31 million blue-collar jobs at the end of the decade, two million more than at the beginning.[26]

A new computerized method of matching jobs with available workers offers hope of reducing unemployment. A Labor Department "Job Bank" is operating in some 50 cities and regions across the country, listing and describing all job offerings in the area of a local employment office of the Manpower Administration.

It can be argued that technical improvements in job-finding, important as they are, can only help reduce the extent of unemployment. They do not go to the cause of it. Some economists say that not enough is known about the impact of fiscal and monetary policy or about the techniques of ending long-term "structural" unemployment. But no government can afford to await the perfection of economic theory before it takes action. It has been the American experience that when unemployment rises, government must act.

---

[25] Department of Labor, *U.S. Manpower in the 1970s* (1970). See "Status of Women," *E.R.R.*, 1970 Vol. II, pp. 573-577.

[26] See "Blue-Collar America," *E.R.R.*, 1970 Vol. II, pp. 635-638.

Jobs for the future

by

William Gerber

1 9 6 9
Dec. 10

JOBS FOR THE FUTURE

YOUNG PEOPLE entering the world of work in the next decade will have had, on the average if present trends continue, a sharply increased number of years of education. And they will expect to obtain jobs which provide not only security and status but also stimulation, outlets for creativity, and opportunities for frequent advancement. The aspirations of the restless new generation will confront society with the task of trying to ensure sufficient job openings despite the economy's ability to get more work done with fewer workers; and there will be need to try also to provide the new labor-force entrants with an exciting atmosphere in which to work.

Along with extended education for the many, the 1970s will see continuance, if not intensification, of the school dropout problem in the inner city. Dropouts will have a particularly hard time because youths under 18 or 20 years of age are virtually excluded from meaningful employment in a country which expects young people to remain in school.[1] It will therefore be important to find new ways to encourage dropouts to take special training in line with their capacities and with the requirements of employers.

In the context of rapid technological and social changes in the world of work, the question often is asked, For what should we be educating our young people? This question applies as much to those who remain in school as to those who drop out and need special training. Competent observers, without belittling the value of the humanities, contend that many aspects of today's curriculum are not in keeping with the times. They think the educational system lags seriously behind changes in social values and structures. According to one investigator, teachers do not know how to relate their subject "to the rest of knowledge, as well as to life." He points out that "In large part, this is what our student rebels

---

[1] See "Jobs for Young People," *E.R.R.*, 1961 Vol. II, pp. 505-509.

are complaining about: . . . relevance."[2] It is widely believed, moreover, that the system of occupational guidance in schools and colleges is inadequate and out of date.

To give the country's young people better preparation for earning a livelihood, to make counseling in the choice of a vocation available to many more of them than at present, and to assure job openings commensurate with their abilities and interests are pivotal tasks for the years ahead. The political fortunes of the Nixon administration may depend not only on disentanglement from the conflict in Viet Nam, but also on the availability of job opportunities and on the effectiveness of programs for manpower training and job placement. A manpower expert has pointed out that the number of men and women entering the labor force in the decade ending in 1975 will show "the largest . . . upturn for a ten-year period in our history."[3]

Educational Background of New Job-Seekers

As far as classroom training is concerned, the level of achievement of Americans coming of age is rising steadily. Recipients of bachelor's or advanced degrees at American colleges and universities in the 10 years from 1969 to 1978 are expected to number around 8.5 million, compared with 4.9 million in the preceding 10-year period. Virtually all of these graduates, other than those who enter the Armed Forces, continue studying, or become housewives, will join the labor force.

The relationship of an advanced degree to success in business was indicated by a survey which the magazine *Careers Today* conducted, over a year ago, among 230 company presidents and 1,500 executives of 500 large concerns. Some 21 per cent of the men at the top, at that time, had earned doctorates, and it was expected that the figure would reach 30 per cent within a year. Of those who had achieved the most rapid advancement, 75 per cent had combined a master's degree in business administration with an undergraduate degree in science or engineering.

About 400,000 of today's undergraduates are black. They constitute 6 per cent of the college population, whereas

---

[2] Charles E. Silberman, quoted in the *New York Times*, Jan. 26, 1969, p. 48. See also "Reorganization of the Universities," *E.R.R.*, 1968 Vol. II, pp. 605-606.

[3] Seymour L. Wolfbein (Temple University), *The Emerging Labor Force; A Strategy for the Seventies* (1969), p. 4.

Jobs for the Future

PROJECTION OF DEGREES AWARDED
IN SELECTED YEARS

	Bachelor's and first professional degrees	Master's degrees	Doctorates (excluding M.D.s)
1968	685,000	148,800	22,200
1969	749,000	160,000	25,100
1970	746,000	190,400	26,500
1972	785,000	212,000	29,200
1974	860,000	226,900	38,900
1976	931,000	253,200	40,600
1978	980,000	273,700	43,900

SOURCE: U. S. Office of Education, *Projections of Educational Statistics to 1977-78* (1969), p. 31. Based on assumption that ratio of degrees to population will continue the 1958-66 trend.

Negroes make up 11.5 per cent of the total population. The number of nonwhite college students has increased dramatically in the past two years, but the level of educational attainment in the black population as a whole is distinctly lower than that of whites. Among persons 25 years old or older in 1967, 20.2 per cent of the Negroes as against 32.8 per cent of the whites were high school graduates; and 4 per cent of the Negroes as against 10.6 per cent of the whites were college graduates. Industry recently has launched vigorous efforts to recruit black college graduates.

The current generation of college graduates is spirited, socially conscious, and given to unconventional thinking. William S. Rukeyser, an associate editor of *Fortune*, has written of those who enter the business world:

> Educated people are bringing impressive skills to business, and making equally impressive demands. Companies wise enough to accommodate to both are reaping profits. But along the way they have had to up-end everything from training programs and organization charts to salary scales and the way top executives allocate their time. . . . Young employees are demanding that they be given productive tasks to do from the first day of work and that the people they work for notice and react to their performance.

Rukeyser added: "This is disturbing bureaucratic peace in some companies, but the results could be beneficial all around." [4]

Preponderance of Openings in Service Sector

The kinds of work available to tomorrow's high school or college graduates and other job-seekers will differ significantly from work being done today. The differences result

---

[4] William S. Rukeyser, "How Youth Is Reforming the Business World," *Fortune*, January 1969, pp. 77-79.

from advancing technology, increased education, and changing values. Technology creates new occupations, raises the demand for people in some lines of work, and reduces the demand in others. Expanded education multiplies job openings for teachers, educational administrators, and producers of educational materials. Changes in values have stimulated demand for travel agents, bus drivers, entertainers, waiters, barmaids, artists, engineers, doctors, and baby-sitters.

The latest Dictionary of Occupational Titles (published by the U. S. Department of Labor in two volumes in 1965) lists 21,741 separate occupations from able seaman to zylomounter (mounter of lenses in zylo-plastic eyeglass frames). The occupations in which demand is growing fastest are those involving work with people and ideas; that is, nonproduction jobs, rather than the goods-producing work of agriculture, mining, manufacturing, and construction.[5]

On an unidentified day in 1956, a celebrated breakthrough occurred in the United States, when two lines of occupational growth—production jobs and nonproduction jobs—crossed. On that day, for the first time in any modern country, more people were employed in nonproduction (white-collar or service) jobs than in production (blue-collar or farm) jobs. "Service employment," as noted by the Chase Manhattan Bank, "accounts for 88 per cent of total employment growth in the postwar period." [6]

The shift to service work results in part from applications of technology which enable farms and factories to produce a larger output with the same number of workers or with fewer workers. This development raises a question that is still unsettled: whether automation and other advances in technology lead to unemployment for the less educated, by abolishing more manual jobs (usually production jobs) than they create and by shifting the emphasis to white-collar work.[7] Some economists contend that availability of jobs, whether for the less educated or the better educated, depends primarily not on technology but on such factors as strong

[5] "Nonproduction jobs" include (1) all jobs in the non-goods-producing sectors of the economy; namely, transportation, communication, trade, finance, government, education, medicine, law, advertising, and others; and (2) nonproduction jobs (those of executives, clerks, salesmen, etc.) in the goods-producing sectors; namely, agriculture, mining, manufacturing, and construction.

[6] "Services in the U. S. Economy," *Business in Brief* (bank newsletter), February 1969, p. 5.

[7] See "Cushioning of Automation," *E.R.R.*, 1963 Vol. II, pp. 781-782.

Jobs for the Future

PROSPECTIVE CHANGES IN EMPLOYMENT
(per cent distribution)

	1960	1980
Goods-producing jobs	(40.8)	(33.2)
Manufacturing	25.6	22.6
Agriculture	8.7	3.6
Construction	5.6	6.5
Mining	0.9	0.5
Service-producing jobs	(59.2)	(66.8)
Trade	19.6	19.0
Services	17.0	22.0
Government	11.8	16.0
Transportation, communications, public utilities	6.4	4.4
Finance, insurance, real estate	4.4	5.4

SOURCE: Edgar L. Morphet and Charles O. Ryan (eds.), *Prospective Changes in Society by 1980* (1966), p. 99.

consumer purchasing power, expanding industrial demand, and economic growth.

School-to-Work Transition; Foreign Experience

James Bryant Conant, former president of Harvard University, commented some years ago on the role of education not only in directing youths to areas of employment where demand exists, but also in facilitating their changeover from school to work: "The educational experiences of youth should fit their subsequent employment. There should be a smooth transition from full-time schooling to a full-time job, whether the transition be after grade 10 or after graduation from high school, college, or university." [8]

A serious disparity exists between the ideal transition mentioned by Conant and the actuality. A Cornell University sociologist has written: "One of the most definitive characteristics of the occupational nature of the urbanized society is the conspicuous absence of apparent mechanisms for communicating occupational knowledge and equating occupations with interests and abilities." [9] The 1968 Manpower Report of the President to Congress outlined the deficiencies as follows:

Eight of 10 school dropouts have never had counseling by school or employment office officials about training or employment opportunities, and 4 out of 10 high school graduates have never had such counseling. There are no school counselors at all in 13 per cent of the nation's secondary schools and in 90 per cent of its elementary schools. . . . Even smaller proportions have been exposed to supervised work experience while in school. Among out-of-school youth in

[8] James Bryant Conant, *Slums and Suburbs* (1961), p. 40.
[9] Lee Taylor, *Occupational Sociology* (1968), p. 189.

147

<small>Comparison of Unemployment Rates</small>

*(Ratio of unemployment rate for youths in two age groups
to unemployment rate for persons aged 25 years or over)*

	Aged 15 to 19	Aged 20 to 24
United States	5.00*	2.19
Italy	4.48	3.13
France	3.71	1.41
Sweden	2.60	1.27
Japan	2.14	1.43

* Unemployment rate in this case, for example, is five times as great as that among workers aged 25 or over.

Source: Franz A. Groemping, *Transition From School to Work in Selected Countries* (1969), p. 34.

1963, only 7 per cent of high school graduates and 3 per cent of dropouts had such work experience.

Numerous books and pamphlets describing the various occupations are available, but "The existing career literature is uniformly sloppy," in the opinion of Peter M. Sandman, author of *Unabashed Career Guide*.[10] Books and materials on specific occupations, Sandman found, stress only the attractive aspects of each occupation. The U. S. Department of Labor, however, attempts to present balanced descriptions in its *Occupational Outlook Handbook* (1968).

Youths in Western Europe and Japan have much less difficulty than American youths in crossing the bridge from school to work, as indicated in the accompanying table. The smoother school-work transition in the places mentioned is due in part to the prevalence there of a number of work-oriented practices. Among these practices are early exposure of school children to varieties of work, through visits and school-supervised work assignments; extensive vocational counseling; enrollment of students, upon completion of their compulsory schooling, in public vocational training programs or an apprenticeship; flexible administration of vocational schools, with adaptations to technological change; and financial help from the government for apprenticeship or on-the-job training.

Herbert Bienstock, a Department of Labor official, commented recently on the superiority of foreign vocational guidance. "It is a strange paradox," he wrote, "that in other nations, where the social and economic institutions are less complex than in the United States, we find the vocational

---

[10] Quoted in *Careers Today*, February 1969, p. 62.

guidance arts to be more highly developed. It would seem that the reverse would—and surely should—be true." [11]

Not all of the methods used abroad in facilitating the transition from school to work are applicable in the United States. For one thing, vocational training in foreign countries reflects, as the President's 1968 Manpower Report stated, "a heavily structured status system for entry into jobs—the kind of system that has been traditionally rejected in the United States." Nevertheless, the shortage in the United States of skilled mechanics and repairmen has been due in part to a mistake not generally made by the Europeans. Philip H. Abelson, editor of *Science,* wrote in the issue of Aug. 16, 1968: "One of our greatest mistakes has been to accord special prestige to a college degree while displaying indifference toward quality in craftsmanship. We reward verbal skill and abstract reasoning and deny dignity to manual workers."

Evolution of Today's Job Structure

THIS COUNTRY, from colonial times to about 1870, was primarily an agricultural society. The principal economic activities were farming, forestry, the fur trade, and fisheries (including whaling). In 1800, more than nine-tenths of the American people made at least a part of their living from farming. Venturesome, literate, and ingenious farmers brought large areas under cultivation. The number of square miles of new farmland added to the total rose steadily from 65,000 in the decade of the 1790s to 215,000 in the 1840s. Farming was the occupation of nearly two-thirds of working Americans in 1850.

American farmers differed from Old World peasants in being mentally energetic, mobile, and eager to adopt new methods. The impact of technology on farming as an occupation began early in American history. Eli Whitney's invention in 1793 of the cotton gin, a device for separating fiber from seed, more than trebled the amount of cotton that could be processed in a day. Chiefly as a result of Whitney's invention, the American cotton crop increased from 1.5 million

---

[11] Herbert Bienstock, "The Transition to Work Here and Abroad: Do U. S. Youth Fare Worse?" *New Generation,* Winter 1969, p. 5.

pounds in 1790 to 85 million pounds in 1810. The cotton gin also stimulated extension of the plantation system and Negro slavery in the South. The individualistic, frontier-pushing farmer sought his fortune in the mid-West and the West rather than the South.

To provide training for the sons of American farmers, Rep. Justin S. Morrill (Whig Vt.) introduced in 1857 the first bill providing for state-administered land-grant colleges. The bill failed to pass. After several further attempts, Morrill's initiative finally led to the enactment, July 2, 1862, of a law donating extensive public lands to the states and territories for establishment of colleges. In the words of the law, "the leading object" of the land-grant colleges "shall be, without excluding other scientific and classical studies, and including military tactics, to teach such branches of learning as are related to agriculture and the mechanic arts, in such manner as the legislatures of the states may respectively prescribe, in order to promote the liberal and practical education of the industrial classes in the several pursuits and professions in life."

Rise of Employment in Industry and Services

The opening of vast areas to farming paved the way for growth of large urban centers of trade and industry in the mid-West and the West, while the industrial revolution was causing rapid expansion of cities in the East and the South. About the time of the Civil War and immediately thereafter, the rate of introduction of new inventions rose markedly, and projects to exploit hitherto unused natural resources also showed notable increases. Numerous companies were formed in the post-bellum period to develop petroleum, aluminum, steel, and the use of electricity. The proportion of jobs in farming declined to 40 per cent in 1900 and plummeted thereafter to about 4.3 per cent in 1969. From about 1900, the absolute number of farm jobs also fell off gradually.

The proportion of American workers engaged in production of goods (agriculture and industry combined) rose steadily until about 1950 but has since declined. Thus, just as agriculture over a period of decades gave way to industry (including mining and construction), so industry began about mid-century to give way to government, education, and other white-collar or service functions.

Jobs for the Future

DISTRIBUTION OF THE LABOR FORCE
(per cent)

	About 1910	About 1930	About 1950	About 1962
United States				
Agriculture	31	22	12	9
Industry	31	31	35	33
Service	38	47	53	59
United Kingdom				
Agriculture	12	6	5	4
Industry	43	43	47	48
Service	45	51	48	48
Germany				
Agriculture	34	29	23	14
Industry	26	30	33	38
Service	26	30	33	38

SOURCE: *International Encyclopedia of the Social Sciences* (1968), Vol. 5, p. 50.

That the United States is not unique in the move to service occupations is shown in the accompanying table comparing distribution of the labor force in this country and in two West European countries. Leon Greenberg, of the U.S. Bureau of Labor Statistics, doubts that the trend to service occupations will accelerate. He told an international conference on automation, at Oberhausen, Germany, in March 1968: "Employment in service producing industries as a per cent of total employment has risen about 3 percentage points every five years since 1947. . . . Projections indicate that the average five-year rise to 1975 will be slightly less—about 2.5 points." These projections suggest, Greenberg concluded, "that we need not be concerned with an acceleration in the shift from goods to services, at least for the next 10 years."

Job Security and Ideal of Full Employment

Working in the right kind of job, a job that suits one's abilities, interests, and aspirations, is vitally important. At times, however, it is even more important just to have a job—some way to earn a living. European governments early in the present century began to provide financial assistance to persons who had trouble in finding a job. In the United States, provision for unemployment insurance was made for the first time in the Social Security Act of 1935. That act became law in a year when 20 per cent of the labor force was without work.[12] As recently as July 9, 1969, President Nixon asked Congress to extend unemployment insurance to the

[12] See "Unemployment Benefits in Times of Prosperity," *E.R.R.*, 1965 Vol. I, pp. 163-164.

small proportion of workers still not covered—mainly workers in firms with only a handful of employees, nonprofit organizations, and state institutions.

Under the influence of Keynesian economics, the idea gained currency during the Great Depression of the 1930s that governments bore responsibility not only for providing subsistence payments to the unemployed, but also for so directing the economy that jobs would be plentiful. A report by Lord Beveridge in 1944, *Full Employment in a Free Society*, and the Employment Act adopted by Congress in February 1946 were milestones toward general acceptance of that idea. The U.N. General Assembly's Universal Declaration of Human Rights, Dec. 10, 1948, stated in Article 23: "Everyone has the right to work, to free choice of employment, to just and favorable conditions of work and to protection against unemployment."

Programs To Help the Disadvantaged Get Jobs

More than 5 per cent of the American labor force was unemployed in 1960, but in the same year more than 10 per cent of nonwhites were out of work. Concern for impoverished Negroes, Puerto Ricans, and Mexican-Americans, with special regard to their high rate of unemployment, led to initiation by the federal government of a number of special job-training and work-experience programs. These programs helped hundreds of thousands of ghetto dwellers and others, but although the unemployment rate for all workers had fallen below 4 per cent by 1968, it was still twice as high for nonwhites.

The first programs aimed to help deprived groups to get jobs were established under the Manpower Development and Training Act of March 15, 1962. This act authorized expenditures by the government for training and employing youths 16 to 21 years of age and for upgrading the skills of those whose old skills had been left behind by technology.[13] During the 1968 presidential campaign, Richard M. Nixon criticized the administration of the act, pledged that he would introduce improvements, and proposed that a National Computer Job Bank be set up to match job openings with persons seeking employment, anywhere in the country. The Department of Labor in September 1969 contracted with a private organization to conduct a pilot program of computerized

---

[13] See Congressional Quarterly's *Congress and the Nation* (Vol. II 1969), pp. 737-743.

matching of unemployed persons with job vacancies, to be expanded if it proves effective.

As part of President Johnson's war on poverty, the Economic Opportunity Act of Aug. 20, 1964, sought to eliminate barriers to employment of disadvantaged persons through neighborhood-oriented and youth-oriented work-experience and training programs.[14] "Possibly the most imaginative development in the creation of job opportunities for the disadvantaged," according to Prof. Garth L. Mangum of George Washington University, "has been the concept of employing the poor to serve the poor in the Community Action Program." Under that program, some 40,000 low-income persons were "involved as teacher aides in education and day care activities, clerical aides, neighborhood aides who visit homes, bars and other places to reorient persons eligible for available services, counseling aides and employment aides who assist professionals in counseling, job development and placement." [15]

Future Changes in Employment Picture

NINE-TENTHS of the scientists and engineers who ever lived are alive today, according to a widely accepted estimate. They are enlarging the frontiers of understanding about man and his world, and developing techniques for manipulating nature, at a geometric rate of progression. As the discoveries and innovations of these creative minds proliferate, the knowledge explosion steadily erodes the theoretical education and the professional or technical skills of a generation of workers. Not only methods but also basic concepts are constantly being outdated and replaced by others.[16]

A study group established by the General Electric Co. in 1968 found that, after an initial period of formal education, "the process of learning and re-training is expected to continue throughout a person's career, leading to new programs and new relationships between business, unions, govern-

---

[14] *Ibid.*, p. 750.

[15] Garth L. Mangum, "Government as Employer of Last Resort," in Sar A. Levitan and others (eds.), *Towards Freedom from Want* (1968), p. 147.

[16] See "Retraining for New Jobs," *E.R.R.*, 1962 Vol. II, pp. 777-778.

ments, schools and universities to institutionalize this proc-ess." [17] Prof. James R. Bright of Harvard's Graduate School of Business Administration has warned that manual workers are not the only ones who will need refresher training:

> If technological advances are going to come more rapidly, be more severe, and differ widely from what has gone before, it follows that education and reeducation must take place at frequent intervals. The factory worker will need to be taught a new skill. The manager and engineer must acquire a working knowledge of new technology and analytical approaches. [18]

That the manager and the engineer will need to be particu-larly flexible is suggested by Auren Uris of the Research Institute of America. He has predicted: "In the business world of the future, experience will be a dirty word. In almost every case, a previous or 'old' way of doing things will be unacceptable." [19]

Some observers believe that new technology and changing social mores will require the average worker to change jobs more than once, perhaps several times, during his working life. Surprisingly, recent reports indicate that occasionally even scientists may need to learn a new trade. Reductions in federal programs of research and development during 1969 led Bryce Nelson to report that the job market in chemistry and other sciences was tightening. He wrote that "Unless the tendency to cut back on federal science spending is reversed, it may well be that the scientific profession will be winnowed to those able scientists who are driven primarily by love of their work." [20]

Nevertheless, it is expected there will be growing short-ages of many types of personnel, especially in the professions, in the coming decade. Medical schools, noted the *Morgan Guaranty Survey* of November 1969, turn out about 9,000 doctors annually. This is only half of the number needed each year to keep up with health needs of a growing population that is expected to total 228 million by 1980—a gain of about 24 million above the U. S. population in 1969. The *Survey* added:

> Workers outside of the professions also will be in tight supply in the coming decade. Rebuilding urban areas of the nation alone would require an added 7,000 carpenters each year, yet in recent years the

[17] General Electric Co., *Our Future Business Environment* (1968), p. 18.

[18] James R. Bright, "Technology, Business, and Education," in Walter J. Ong (ed.), *Knowledge and the Future of Man; International Symposium* (1968), p. 211.

[19] Auren Uris, "Executives of the Future," *Nation's Business*, January 1969, p. 69.

[20] Bryce Nelson, "A Surplus of Scientists? The Job Market Is Tightening," *Science*, Oct. 31, 1969, p. 582.

number of carpenters in the U.S. has actually declined by 50,000, according to one manpower study. Even unskilled laborers are expected to be increasingly scarce in most areas of the country as industry and government training programs steadily reduce the "hard core" unemployed. From all indications, the do-it-yourself trend for the American homeowner is not to disappear in the seventies.

Labor-force growth in the 1970s is expected to increase at a 1.7 per cent annual rate, slightly higher than the indicated growth rate of 1.6 per cent for the decade of the sixties.

Effects of Automation on Attitude of Workers

In old and new locations, personnel managers and other administrators are devoting increased attention to the satisfaction or dissatisfaction which the jobs in their establishments provide for the intellectual and manual workers there. In a labor market in which advanced skills are in short supply, employers are eager to husband the loyalty of their most capable workers. In this connection, the feeling is growing that to the greatest possible extent jobs should be fitted to individual talents; that is, that the work to be done should be structured in accordance with the interests and aptitudes of the workers, as against the older idea that jobs are what they are, and the only problem of placement is to find a round peg for a round hole.

Michael Silva, discussing the impact of tomorrow's college graduate on the world of business, has written: "A new wave of Americans, with more affluence and education than ever before, will be creating their own jobs in large companies instead of filling slots as many do today. With necessities like food and fun assured as a right, the post-affluents will demand and get careers free of slavishness, and do work that is more like play." [21] A 1969 survey of recruiters for business concerns indicated that college graduates today appear less concerned with income than with other job satisfactions, including company participation in community affairs and public service.[22] The director of manpower utilization of the American Telephone & Telegraph Co. jestingly envisions workers "picketing their employer with placards that read: We demand meaningful work. We want to be plugged in. We demand responsibility." [23]

---

[21] Michael Silva, "The Mass Elite," *Careers Today*, Charter Issue, 1968, p. 80.

[22] "Amid Campus Unrest, Graduates Rush for Jobs," *U.S. News and World Report*, April 7, 1969, pp. 49-51.

[23] Robert N. Ford, "The Obstinate Employee," *Psychology Today*, November 1969, p. 33.

Investigators have found that, in an office or shop where the work has been computerized, the new situation contains elements of both increased and decreased satisfaction for the workers. Machines have taken over the tasks which are less pleasant and more strenuous; workers tend to have greater physical mobility on the job and more frequent contact with the technical staff; and there is often increased opportunity for exercise of judgment. Counterbalancing these advantages are the faster tempo, lack of control over the pace of the work, necessity for constant alertness and close concentration, and the heavy burden of responsibility imposed by awareness of the serious consequences of an error. Sometimes boredom also is in evidence.

New Concepts of Work, Leisure, and Creativity

Experts are not agreed on how soon, if ever, society will be able to turn over most of its work to machines. Arnold J. Toynbee is confident that such a time will come. "The accelerating advance of technology is carrying us towards a novel state of society," he has said. "We are all going to be paid high wages for working for only a few hours in the week." [24] Kent D. Shinbach, an American medical researcher, has ventured a time estimate:

> Within 40 years only one-fourth of the population will be involved in what we now call work. And this involvement will usually amount to a 24-hour work week. . . . Jobs and workers will eventually be known as outmoded concepts from our mechanical heritage. . . . All of us who anticipate, cherish, and celebrate the weekend are probably among the last adherents of a fading cult. [25]

Joseph N. Froomkin and others hold a different view: "The prospects of a utopia, or a Calvinist hell, where work will become redundant, are not likely to face Western society in the near future. Historically, periods of increases in productivity have been followed by periods of stagnation in the rate of increase in productivity." [26] According to Peter F. Drucker, "The report of the demise of work is not only premature; it is false. Indeed the trend runs the other way. Work is growing faster than the work force and is likely to continue to grow faster." [27]

---

[24] Arnold J. Toynbee, *Change and Habit; The Challenge of Our Times* (1966), p. 218.

[25] Kent D. Shinbach, "Technology and Social Change: Choosing a Near Future," *Mental Hygiene,* April 1968, p. 281.

[26] Joseph N. Froomkin (Department of Health, Education, and Welfare), "Automation," in the *International Encyclopedia of the Social Sciences* (1968), Vol. I, p. 487.

[27] Peter F. Drucker, "Worker and Work in the Metropolis," *Daedalus,* Fall 1968, p. 1243.

A manpower study by the National Planning Association indicates that to achieve national goals would require by 1975 the employment of 10 million more persons than are expected to be in the labor force at that time.[28] Analysts in the Bureau of Labor Statistics also doubt that any trend toward drastic reduction of the world's work has begun. That planners and administrators at least will have more work to do in the future than they do now, is suggested by a summary of recent literature on technology and work which noted that, according to most predictions, "while workers will increasingly have free time, the upper echelons will not." [29]

The so-called Puritan concept considers work as unavoidable and arduous, as a duty, and as dealing with things. A comparable idea, that work is necessary for the normal functioning of human beings, was held by Sigmund Freud. A recent student of the subject pointed out:

> The most important function of work is to enable us to use our capacities to the full. Aristotle, over 2,000 years ago, pinpointed the issue with unparalleled clarity. The essence of happiness, he argued, is doing the best we can with the talents we have. . . . People will have to discover personal or social goals which they feel worthy of serious effort. This will require new attitudes, and education will have to create them.[30]

While many statesmen and economists are striving to find ways of increasing paid employment and thus reducing unemployment, Robert Theobald feels that society has an obligation to promote, through applications of technology, the fullest amount of unemployment—that is, freedom from the necessity for regular, prolonged periods of work. Theobald asserts that society should, at the same time, develop "financial mechanisms that enable the individual to act as an institution, self-directed, and alone responsible for his activities." Schools and universities should "develop creativity and enlarge the capacity of the individual to think in terms of his own uniqueness." [31]

The human race itself, Victor C. Ferkiss believes, is "on the threshold of self-transfiguration, of attaining new powers over itself and its environment that can alter its nature as fundamentally as walking upright or the use of tools." [32]

---

[28] Leonard A. Lecht, *Manpower Needs for National Goals in the 1970s* (1969).

[29] Harvard University Program on Technology and Society, *Technology and Work* (Winter 1969), p. 8.

[30] Hans P. Rickman, *Living With Technology* (1967), pp. 84-85, 90.

[31] Robert Theobald, "Should Men Compete With Machines?" *The Nation,* May 9, 1966, pp. 546, 548.

[32] Victor C. Ferkiss, *Technological Man: The Myth and the Reality* (1969), p. 6.

Ferkiss views the American astronauts as forerunners of this new, creative species, "technological man." In the dawning civilization which he envisions, semi-skilled and unskilled labor might still play a large part in the economy but have little share in the job satisfactions afforded the scientific elite. Pursuits which observers believe likely to play an important role in the future organization of work and leisure include voluntary study, artistic creation, and religion.[33]

Individual Freedom and Plans for Manpower Use

For the near future, when work for pay will still be an urgent reality, social theorists face the problem of trying to harmonize manpower planning and individual freedom. Eli Ginzberg of Columbia University has highlighted the problem:

> There is an inherent antagonism between placing high value on the freedom of the individual to choose his work and to select his employer and the thrust of manpower planning which aims at influencing, even directing, the choices that people make about their future occupations and the decisions they reach about current employment. . . . But we know that one man's freedom may be another's fetters. . . . [For example, in declining employment areas such as agriculture,] if nothing is done to help the young, freedom may prove to be, as in Anatole France's parable, only the freedom to go hungry.[34]

Several kinds of governmental action affecting manpower have come to be regarded as consistent with individual freedom. Among them are stimulation of job-producing business expansion through loans or special tax incentives and through increases of consumer purchasing power in the form of higher social security payments or lower taxes; provision of opportunities for vocational training and of funds for subsistence while undergoing training; and expenditures for public works to provide jobs as well as to serve other social purposes.

Some economists favor, as a job-producing measure, substantial reduction of the over-all length of time worked by members of the labor force—through extension of schooling, shortening of the work-week, lengthening of vacations, and early retirement. Simple reduction of the work-week has been ineffectual in the past as a device to increase jobs, for employers often have preferred to pay current employees at

---

[33] See "Leisure in the Great Society," *E.R.R.*, 1964 Vol. II, pp. 914-919.
[34] Eli Ginzberg, *Manpower Agenda for America* (1968), p. 242.

overtime rates rather than to hire additional workers. Furthermore, when the work-week is shortened, some workers take on second jobs.

Edwin F. Shelley, president of an engineering firm, has suggested "a national system of Earned Educational Leave," adjustable to the rate of unemployment. Thus, if 5 per cent of the workers were unemployed, he would remove 5 per cent of the labor force for a year, "for refreshment of skills, knowledge, and personal outlook"; if 10 per cent were unemployed, a like percentage would be assigned to educational leave; and so forth, with financing of the costs shared by business and government.[35]

Individual freedom is not infringed upon by government correlation of information about areas of declining or rising demand and supply or by provision of guidance and other forms of assistance to bring jobs and workers together. In all such programs, it is important for organs of government to avoid the opposite evils—the Scylla and Charybdis—of (1) overzealously requiring people to choose, prepare for, and work at jobs arbitrarily determined to be appropriate, and (2) inadequately guiding, advising, and assisting persons who are, or will be, in the market for jobs. In looking ahead into the decade of the 1970s one observation can be made with safety: the jobs that pay the best and are the most satisfying will go to those who are best prepared by reason of education and training.

---

[35] Edwin F. Shelley, "Earned Educational Leave: A Proposal," in Juanita M. Kreps (ed.), *Technology, Manpower, and Retirement Policy* (1966), pp. 193-194.

LEISURE BUSINESS

by

Ralph C. Deans

1 9 7 3
Feb. 28

LEISURE BUSINESS

M ASS LEISURE is both a promise and problem in modern society. It is said that Americans are moving toward the carefree Polynesian pattern of life, devoting less and less of their lives to the workshop and more and more to the pursuit of pleasure. This line of thinking draws impressive support from statistical evidence compiled by government and business on hours worked, dollars earned and money spent. It is also said that Americans have no knack for the true enjoyment of leisure and fill their new-found free time in boredom or recreational consumerism. But if increased leisure is a mixed blessing in the eyes of social scientists and a cause of concern to environmentalists, it is a bonanza for a growing segment of American business known as the "Good Life Industry."

Collectively, Americans spend billions on the "Good Life" every year and the amount is increasing. The *Forbes* magazine Annual Report on American Industry, a general investment guide, describes the recreation business as a "fast growth area." There are several reasons why this is so. Aside from the fact that Americans have the time for recreation, they also have the money and the mobility to enjoy it. As *Forbes* noted, there is something compulsive about the way Americans spend money on recreation: "Free time unused is almost a sin. To be transformed into leisure time, it must be used, it must be filled to overflowing."[1]

The "Good Life Industry" is enormous. A list of the goods and services people buy for recreation is endless. They range from snowmobiles to swimwear, from the drinks consumed at a "singles" bar to a second home in the country, from needlework materials to pleasure yachting, from camping in the wilderness to playing roulette in Las Vegas, and from ballet to boxing. The Economic Unit of *U.S. News & World Report* estimated early in 1972 that during the year "spending on spare-time activities" would total $105 billion—more than is spent for national defense or the construction of new homes.[2]

---

[1] *Forbes*, Jan. 1, 1973, p. 187.
[2] "Leisure Boom: Biggest Ever and Still Growing," *U.S. News & World Report*, April 17, 1972, p. 42.

The Department of Commerce makes an annual estimate of leisure expenditures, invariably far less than industry estimates. In its most recent survey, for 1971, the department estimated that Americans spent more than $42 billion on 12 categories of recreational activities. They were:

Books and maps	$3.7 billion	Radio and TV repair	$1.3 billion
Magazines, news-papers and sheet music	$4.5 billion	Flowers, seeds and potted plants	$1.6 billion
Nondurable toys and sports supplies	$6.1 billion	Admissions to sports, movies, stage plays, operas, etc.	$2.4 billion
Wheel goods, durable toys, sports equipment, boats and pleasure aircraft	$5.1 billion	Clubs and fraternal organizations	$1.1 billion
		Commercial partici-pant amusements	$1.9 billion
Radio and television sets, records, musical instruments	$9.7 billion	Pari-mutuel net receipts	$1.0 billion
		Other	$3.6 billion

According to department estimates, expenditures on recreation totaled $33.6 billion in 1968, $36.9 billion in 1969, and $40.1 billion in 1970. Not included in the statistics were expenditures on recreational vehicles, second homes, foreign travel, alcoholic beverages, swimming pools and many other goods and services that are leisure-oriented.

In fact, no precise measurement of the leisure business can be made. The purchase and cooking of food, for instance, normally fall under the category of a necessity. Yet the new interest in gourmet cooking,[3] along with related cookbooks and television programing, is at least partly a recreational activity. The manufacture and sale of carpentry tools, once totally unrelated to leisure, today depend largely on the continued strength of the do-it-yourself movement. The scope of the leisure business is further indicated by such statistics as the following: 12.2 million golfers, 4.2 million ski enthusiasts, 37 million bicyclists, 10.7 million tennis players and 1.5 million snowmobile owners in the United States. There are 2 million second homes in the country and that number is growing at the rate of 150,000 to 200,000 a year.

The leisure industry is said to be relatively "recession proof." That is, people continue to purchase leisure goods and services during an economic recession. They may postpone the purchase of a car or refrigerator but are not so likely to delay the purchase of a tennis racket or a set of golf clubs. At the same

---

[3] See "Gourmet Cooking," *E.R.R.*, 1971 Vol. I, pp. 309-324.

time, leisure-oriented companies are under an almost constant reorganization. The industry is a volatile one, partly dependent on fads. A company introducing a new recreational item typically experiences a fast spurt in sales followed by a similarly steep falloff; the item falls out of favor or other companies begin producing rival versions and introduce improvements. John McKelvey, an analyst of the leisure business for the Midwest Research Institute, has written that "even in this huge spending area, more of the companies that serve [the leisure market] lose money than make money."[4]

Wide Range of Leisure Activities in United States

McKelvey wrote that, in terms of time consumed, television viewing is the largest single recreational activity in the United States. According to census findings, 96 per cent of all American homes have at least one television set. And the set is turned on an average of six hours and 18 minutes a day, the 1971 *Broadcasting Yearbook* reported.[5] In terms of expenditure, however, travel is believed to be by far the largest category of leisure activity.

A survey by the National Family Opinion Corp., under the auspices of *Better Homes and Gardens* magazine, suggested that Americans spent $27 billion on domestic vacation and recreational trips in 1971. Travel Editor Gordon Greer told Editorial Research Reports that surveys conducted for the magazine also indicated that the average family took 1.7 trips per year, the average trip lasted 11.9 days and the average per-family expenditure was $404. According to Greer, another survey indicated that most families traveled "for the educational value" of the experience.

Other estimates suggest that expenditures on domestic vacations amount to $40 billion or more a year, along with an estimated $7.5 billion spent abroad in 1972. McKelvey reported that the growth of the motel business was "staggering." It is estimated, he said, that more than 6,500 major facilities are in operation and have in excess of 675,000 rooms available. "And the occupancy rates are good, around 65 per cent on the average," he added.

According to the Midwest Research Institute, water-oriented activities provide the leisure industry its area of fastest growth. The estimated number of swimming pools, private

---

[4] John McKelvey, "Fun and Games in the U.S.," *MRI Quarterly* (a publication of the Midwest Research Institute), spring 1972, p. 6.

[5] The amount of time spent watching television is reportedly increasing. A. C. Nielsen statistics indicate that the average viewing time during the winter of 1972-73 reached an all-time peak of about seven hours a day.

and public, increased from 133,000 in 1958 to more than one million today. Maintenance costs for the pools are calculated at $150 million a year. Boating has undergone a similar surge in popularity. There are 43 million boat owners in the country who spend $4 billion a year on their craft, according to the institute's calculations. But again the "product mix" is continually changing. Water skiing, once a minor activity, is on the increase while surfing, once extremely popular, has fallen off.

Camping and hiking provide businessmen with another large and growing market. According to MRI, Americans spent nearly $2 billion a year on tents, packs and other equipment. *The Wall Street Journal* reported that the hiking boot is the footwear industry's "hottest item" these days. "Beginning, as many of these things do, with youths, it now has overtaken the rest of the country. If you keep your head down, you'll spy these bulky boots almost everywhere, from Wall Street to Harvard Yard."[6] Sales of travel trailers, truck campers and motor homes amounted to more than $1 billion in 1970 and are expected to double that figure by the mid-1970s.

The recreational boom has given rise to several types of off-road vehicles, including dune buggies, minibikes and snowmobiles. Invented by Canadian J. A. Bombardier and first marketed in 1959, the snowmobile is becoming increasingly popular. According to the International Snowmobile Industry Association, there are now nearly 1.5 million snowmobiles in the United States. Some 250 major snowmobile races are held around the country, attracting growing numbers of spectators. Automobile drag racing, on the other hand, is apparently on the wane.

One of the more curious recreational success stories is needlepoint—a pastime publicized by needlepoint artist Roosevelt Grier, a former pro football tackle for the Los Angeles Rams. *Business Week* magazine reported that $25 million to $30 million was spent on needlepoint materials in 1972 and the market is increasing at a rate of 30 per cent a year. "The current boom began five years ago when manufacturers brought out canvases with contemporary designs and brightly colored yarns to replace the traditional puce and dusty rose."[7] Bicycling is another long-established leisure activity that has become more popular in recent years, especially with adults. There are more than 37 million cyclists in

---

[6] *The Wall Street Journal*, Jan. 17, 1973.
[7] "Who Makes the Money in Needlepoint," *Business Week*, Dec. 16, 1972, p. 30.

ATTENDANCE AT SPORTS EVENTS

Sport	1959	1972	Point change
Baseball	28%	30%	+ 2
Football	23	33	+10
Basketball	18	23	+ 5
Stock car racing	9	2	− 7
Horse racing	9	10	+ 1
Wrestling	6	7	+ 1
Boxing	4	14	+10
Hockey	4	7	+ 3
Dog racing	2	4	+ 2
Tennis	2	2	—
Track & field	2	6	+ 4
Soccer	1	13	+12

SOURCE: Gallup Poll

the United States; more than 8.5 million bicycles were sold in 1971 alone.

Popularity of Participatory and Spectator Sports

Sports attendance figures in the United States exceeded 59 million in 1972; admissions to major events yielded more than $1 billion during the year. Almost all sports attracted significantly larger numbers of spectators than in 1959, according to a Gallup poll. (See table above.) The survey found that football had overtaken baseball as the nation's favorite spectator sport. As a result of this interest in football, there has been a boom in stadium construction. Ten of the 26 stadiums used by National Football League teams have been built since 1960; eight NFL cities have plans to increase seating capacity.[8]

New ice rinks, even in the Deep South, have made ice skating and ice hockey nationwide sports in recent years. The National Hockey League has expanded since 1966 from 6 teams to 16, and it plans to add 8 more teams in the next few years. League officials credit television coverage for much of the increased interest. The National Broadcasting Company, in its purchase of rights to telecast hockey games in the 1972-73 season, was reported to have paid the league $5.5 million— almost three times more than the Columbia Broadcasting System paid the previous season.

More than 30,000 "serious" skaters are registered in clubs affiliated with the United States Figure Skating Association,

[8] *Pro* (official NFL magazine), Nov. 20, 1972, p. 12b.

167

in addition to the hundreds of thousands—perhaps millions—
"round 'n' rounders" who skate on indoor rinks and frozen
lakes and streams. One reason for the growth in popularity of
ice skating is that blade and boot manufacturers have been
able to give the awkward skater greater stability with improved products.

Swimming is by far the most popular participatory sport.
The Gallup survey indicated that 42 per cent of all Americans
had been swimming at least once during 1972. Although fishing
appears to be losing some of its appeal, it is still America's
second-most popular participatory sport, followed by bowling,
baseball-softball, hunting and golf, in that order. *(See table,
p. 169.)* Ski Industries America reports that there are more
than four million skiers in the United States. They spent more
than $1.3 billion during 1971 on equipment, travel, lift tickets
and entertainment. The 10.7 million American tennis players,
a growing number, are believed to spend $50 million on
rackets, balls and accessories a year. Some 12.5 million golfers
spend an estimated $3 billion a year playing on the country's
10,500 courses.

Factors in Growth of Recreational Expenditures

Perhaps the greatest bulwark of the leisure boom is the affluence of the average American. Total personal income for the
first 10 months of 1972 amounted to nearly $772 billion, an in-
crease of about 9 per cent over the same period of 1971. The
total for 1972 is expected to be more than $920 billion—com-
pared with $861 billion in 1971—when all the figures are in.
The Department of Commerce does not measure "discretion-
ary" income—what is left over after payment for food, bever-
ages, clothing and shelter—because of the difficulty of separating "necessary" expenditures from all the rest. However, "dis-
posable" income—defined as what is left over after payment
of taxes and social security—rose from $2,945 per capita in
1968 to $3,595 in 1971, a gain of 22 per cent. After allowing
for inflation; there was still a gain of almost 8 per cent.

Workers not only have more income but also more
time in which to spend it. They are assured a minimum of
five three-day weekends each year.[9] More than 40 million
now work under conditions of employment entitling them to
three-week vacations. Increases in vacation time are one of the
most important factors contributing to the total amount of free

---

[9] Washington's Birthday, Memorial Day and Veterans Day have been observed on
Mondays since 1971, as stipulated by a federal law. It also established Columbus Day
as a national holiday, to be celebrated on a Monday also. Labor Day has traditionally
been observed on a Monday.

PARTICIPATION IN SPORTS

Sport	Per cent participation		Point change
	1959	1972	
Swimming	33%	42%	+ 9
Fishing	32	24	— 8
Bowling	18	28	+10
Hunting	16	14	— 2
Baseball-Softball	11	19	+ 8
Golf	8	14	+ 6
Ice Skating	6	9	+ 3
Horseback riding	5	10	+ 5
Roller skating	4	5	+ 1
Tennis	4	12	+ 8
Volleyball	4	11	+ 7
Skiing	3	5	+ 2

SOURCE: Gallup Poll

---

time in the United States. "The recent growth in the number of vacation weeks has been spectacular," two analysts for the Bureau of Labor Statistics wrote. "In nine years, from 1960 to 1969, the total number of weeks that workers spent on vacation increased almost 50 per cent, or from 87 [million] to 129 million. The average length of a worker's vacation increased from 1.3 to 1.7 weeks...."[10]

Several other trends have helped to boost the leisure industry, among them the relative youthfulness of the population. *Forbes* magazine commented that "Although the number of 'typical' recreation consumer spenders (ages 25-44) remained fairly static during the Sixties, total personal recreation expenditures went from $19.5 billion in 1961 to over $40 billion in 1971. That age group is expected to expand at a rate of over 2 per cent a year in the Seventies."

Increased life expectancy has been another factor. Life expectancy for men at birth increased by 18 years to almost 67 years between 1900 and 1960, according to the Bureau of Labor Statistics analysts. They wrote that "the net effect of changes in life and worklife expectancy was an increase of nine years of work and nine years of time out of the labor force."[11] Summing up, these researchers found that reduction of the workweek, increased vacation time, more paid holidays, more years of education and retirement had significantly increased the total amount of leisure in the United States.

[10] Geoffrey H. Moore and Janice Neipert Hedges, "Trends in Labor and Leisure," *Monthly Labor Review*, February 1971, p. 5.

[11] *Ibid.*, p. 5.

Gradual Increase of Leisure Time

IN A MEMORANDUM to John Fairfax in 1789, George Washington wrote that he expected maximum effort and output from the slaves and workers on his several plantations. "To request that my people may be at their work as soon as it is light, work till it is dark, and be diligent while they are at it, can hardly be necessary; because the propriety of it must strike every manager who attends to my interest." Dawn to dark working hours were prevalent on farms and in businesses well into the 19th century. Workers in the early 1800s strove for a 10-hour day but the competition for jobs was so fierce that wage earners could not exact conditions from their employers. It is a comment on the lack of leisure time during that era that Massachusetts in 1845 forbade by law the employment of children under 12 for more than 10 hours a day. Earlier, in 1840, President Van Buren declared 10 hours a legal day's work on government projects.

During this time leisure was largely confined to "society" in the eastern cities and the South. "In fact," wrote historian Carl Russel Fish, "few American men had sufficient leisure for much participation in or attendance at games." The rich migrated to summer resort areas in the Northeast while southern families repaired during the summer to family cottages at various Virginia springs. On the western frontier, "Social life was mainly what could be fitted in with the requirements of labor, and was largely connected with neighborly assistance on such occasions as harvesting, house raising, corn huskings and the like."[12]

Leisure was largely confined to Sunday, a day of rest from toil in keeping with the biblical injunction. Blue Laws forbidding commercial activity on Sunday were originally inspired by piety but were sustained, even as the secular spirit became dominant in the United States, by the desire to protect workers from exploitation. Antipathy to working on Sunday is so ingrained in the consciousness that many union contracts typically call for higher pay for working on that day than any other.[13]

The first widespread effort to adopt an eight-hour day was directed by the Federation of Organized Trades and Labor,

[12] Carl Russel Fish, *The Rise of the Common Man* (1927), pp. 148-151.
[13] See "Sunday Selling," *E.R.R.*, 1960 Vol. I, pp. 119-136.

which called a general strike May 1, 1886, to try to achieve that goal. Several hundred thousand workers participated in the work stoppage, but the famous riot in Chicago's Haymarket Square on May 4 discredited the movement. The American Federation of Labor, first organized under that name in 1886, was dedicated from the start to the eight-hour day. It adopted a strategy of giving all-out support to each union that took up the fight. "From 1886 to 1890...the hours-of-work movement... even more than wage issues, converted the unions into practical, hard-hitting organizations dedicated to the improvement of conditions for workers on the job."[14] The strategy worked, first for carpenters, then for miners, bakers and typographers.

Labor Unions' Efforts to Fix Five-Day Standard

The labor movement tried to cut back the hours of the workday rather than the number of days worked. Even as the average workweek in industry declined from an estimated 69.7 hours in 1850 to 47.7 hours in 1930, the six-day week prevailed. "The first known five-day week appeared in the United States as recently as 1908, and was unique for years. A decade later, in 1918, there were only a handful of five-day firms. And in 1929, only 5 per cent of the American labor force was on five-day."[15]

Labor unions never lost interest in fighting for fewer hours of work per week, though they rarely envisioned an increase in leisure time as the goal. In the beginning, labor sought simply to relieve workers of the hardship of the inhumanly long working day. Toward the end of the 19th century, unions took up the rallying cry for an eight-hour day as a means of building up strength and winning members. Still later the demand for a shorter standard workweek became a mechanism for raising wages—by requiring added pay for extra hours.

Long hours continued to prevail in most private employment. The steel industry, manned largely by immigrant labor, did not give up the 12-hour day until 1923. By the end of the 1920s, the eight-hour day with a Saturday half-holiday had become the standard. On the eve of the Depression, the average worker in manufacturing put in 44 hours a week. The average for other workers was closer to 48 hours.

The Davis-Bacon Act of 1931 required companies doing construction work for the government to pay their workers over-

---

[14] George Brooks, "Historical Background," *The Shorter Work Week* (1957), p. 12. See also "Four Day Week," *E.R.R.* 1971 Vol. II, p. 616

[15] Riva Poor, "Reporting a Revolution in Work and Leisure," *4 Days, 40 Hours* (1970), p. 17.

time rates beyond eight hours a day but made no provision for work in excess of 40 hours a week. The Walsh-Healey Act of 1936 imposed both an eight-hour day and a 40-hour-week standard on companies holding government supply contracts of $10,000 or more. The Fair Labor Standards Act of 1938 applied a 44-hour (later 40) standard—but no daily standard—to millions of workers in private business who engaged in interstate commerce or made goods sold in interstate commerce.

Labor unions, including the new industrial unions which were in a period of great growth during the Thirties, tended to follow the statutory model. But even when unions succeeded in negotiating a workweek shorter than 40 hours, the new schedule almost invariably called for shorter rather than fewer work days. When rubber workers in 1936 won a 30-hour week, for example, the work was spread over six days. The wage-hour provisions of the Fair Labor Standards Act were intended to attain the law's objective of eliminating "labor conditions detrimental to the maintenance of the minimum standard of living necessary for the health, efficiency, and general well-being of workers." The overtime pay requirement was viewed as a penalty on employers who went beyond the statutory standard and as an incentive to employ more workers. But in all of this, the unions were concerned with levels of pay, unemployment and membership—not leisure.

Recent Experiments With Shorter Work Week

Fear of heavy unemployment after World War II led to the introduction of several bills in Congress to cut the workweek to 30 hours. The measures, supported by labor, were seen as a way to spread the available work among the mass of returning workers. Anticipated unemployment, however, did not occur and it was not until the 1950s that interest revived in a shorer workweek. At that time, it was fear that automation would throw millions out of work that prompted the demand for a 30-hour week. The American Federation of Labor voted at its 1953 convention to "press vigilantly" toward that goal. And at the convention that united the American Federation of Labor and the Congress of Industrial Organizations in December 1955, the AFL-CIO adopted resolutions calling for shortening the standard 40-hour workweek both through legislation and by collective bargaining.

Among major unions that pledged in 1955-57 to press for a shorter workweek were the United Automobile Workers, the International Association of Machinists, the Textile Workers Union, International Brotherhood of Electrical Workers,

AVERAGE HOURS OF WORK

Year	Average weekly hours of work	Year	Average weekly hours of work
1900	53.2	1950	41.2
1910	52.1	1955	41.6
1920	49.8	1960	40.5
1930	47.7	1965	40.5
1940	43.9	1970	39.6

SOURCE: Bureau of Labor Statistics

---

the Communications Workers Union and the United Steelworkers. Some reduction in working hours was gained through these efforts. The five-day week, however, remained the standard. The four-day week was barely known, and until the late Sixties almost no effort was made to promote it as a suitable norm for the nation.

Curiously enough, the major thrust toward the four-day week came from employers, rather than the unions. When Henry Ford in the early 1920s decided to put his men on a five-day week, he said: "We believe that in order to live properly, every man should have more time to spend with his family." Ford was also upholding the theory that a working class with leisure was necessary if an economically viable balance between production and consumption was to be obtained. This viewpoint gained some adherents in the business community during that decade. President Hoover's Committee on Recent Economic Changes stated in a 1929 report that business was coming to realize "in a practical way...not only that leisure is 'consumable' but that people cannot 'consume' leisure without consuming goods and services, and that leisure which results from an increased man-hour productivity helps to create new needs and new and broader markets."[16]

Over the long haul, a decrease in working time with no loss of pay is made possible by increased productivity. As productivity increased, labor sought and won a share of the gains in the form of higher wages and more time off. In the case of the four-day week, however, employers have sought it in order to improve productivity by introducing more efficient scheduling. In many cases, the output has increased with a shorter work schedule. In some cases, costly problems of absenteeism and rapid turnover have been overcome.

---

[16] Cited in "Hours of Labor," *Encyclopedia of the Social Sciences*, Vol. IV, p. 478.

An estimated 2,000 firms have now swung over to a four-day week. Interest in the movement surged with the publication in November 1970 of *4 Days, 40 Hours*, a symposium reporting on various aspects of the shorter workweek. Most of the chapters were keyed to an account by the book's editor, Riva Poor, on her investigation of 27 companies that had tried some variant of the shorter week. Mrs. Poor, a management consultant, concluded from her studies that "the four-day, 40-hour work-week is spreading in our society—and spreading rapidly." In a survey of the habits of the new leisure class enjoying a 72-hour weekend, Mrs. Poor and statistician James L. Steele found striking increases in travel and recreation. Swimming and boating by the four-day workers increased 319 per cent while hunting and fishing went up 95 per cent.[17]

Debate About How Much Free Time Is Available

Despite the statistical increases in free time, many Americans do not share in it. They may feel that they have little more free time than their parents had, perhaps even less if they commute long distances or if they are women who work and also keep house. The *Harvard Business Review* calculated in its issue of May-June 1969 that factory workers actually had less leisure time in 1967 than in 1939. They were on the job an average of 40.6 hours in 1967, almost three hours more than in 1939—a depression year—and their commutation time from home to factory and back had multiplied. The longer hours indicated a desire for more money to pay for increasingly complex and costly leisure-time pursuits.

Herman Kahn and Anthony J. Siener of the Hudson Institute "think tank" foresee a remarkably similar situation at the end of this century. In *The Year 2000*, they write that the lower middle-class worker will be earning $10,000 to $20,000 (in terms of 1965 dollars) in a year of brief workweeks but "might still wish to increase income by moonlighting...."

Another factor that affects leisure time is how that time is distributed—in bits and pieces or in great chunks of several days together. Marion Clawson and Jack L. Knetch wrote in their study *Economics of Outdoor Recreation*, "Just as the possible use of land may be greatly affected by the size of the parcels into which it is subdivided, so may the use of leisure time be equally affected by the size of the pieces. In each case, excessive subdivision may reduce a total value."[18]

---

[17] Riva Poor and James L. Steele, "The Recreation of People at 4-Day Firms," *4 Days, 40 Hours* (1970), pp. 116-117.

[18] Marion Clawson and Jack L. Knetsch, *Economics of Outdoor Recreation* (1966), p. 14.

In the *Harried Leisure Class* (1970), economist Staffan Burenstam Linder argued that the pace of life is quickening to such an extent that there is a growing scarcity of time. Instead of reaping the fruits of increased productivity in terms of leisure, man is reaping it in terms of consumption—a higher standard of living. Having once made that decision, Linder argues, man is stuck with his material objects and must spend more time servicing them. An example is the camping enthusiast who purchases a camp truck. He must now continue to work in order to pay for the added expense of operating the vehicle on a vacation.

"The very affluence of Americans helps make free time a scarce item," economists at the Morgan Guaranty Trust Company noted in an analysis of "The New Leisure."[19] "A country club membership, for example, means that hours *must* be spent on the facilities if members are to get their money's worth." Gibert Burck of *Fortune* magazine has written that the prospect of a leisure-oriented society is "nonsense or illusion or both." "The basic reason why carefree abundance and leisure are not likely to fall into our laps like ripe fruit may be put very simply. The more time we save in making goods, the more time we spend providing services."[20]

Problems Facing a Leisure Society

WHEN LOOMS WEAVE by themselves man's slavery will end, Aristotle wrote. The philosopher lived in a leisure society based on slave labor and his comment was taken to mean that there would always be a need for workers. Today, technology has created a situation in which the looms do indeed weave by themselves, or nearly so. Yet society has arrived at what many think is the brink of a new era of leisure with trepidation. Western man has glorified work as a good in its own right for so long that it has become a part of his psyche. The philosophical and spiritual underpinning of much of the modern world is based on the conception of work as the expiation of original sin. Psychologists document the fact that many people feel "guilty" unless they work, and work hard.

President Nixon struck a similar note in his 1972 re-election campaign. "The work ethic holds that labor is good in itself;

---

[19] "The New Leisure," *The Morgan Guaranty Survey* (monthly publication of the Morgan Guaranty Trust Company), March 1971, p. 8.

[20] Gilbert Burck, "There'll Be Less Leisure Than You Think," *Fortune*, March 1970, p. 87.

that a man or woman at work not only makes a contribution to his fellow man but becomes a better person by virtue of the act of working." Continuing, Nixon warned: "We are faced with a choice between the work ethic that built this nation's character—and the new welfare ethic that could cause America's character to weaken."

The work ethic obviously remains strongly implanted in the American consciousness. However, automation has debased much of modern-day work without eliminating it. For many plant and clerical employees, work is a series of boring, repetitive actions. This has led to economic growth and progress but work, growth and progress are all becoming anathema to many Americans. Management expert Gordon F. Bloom wrote that "it is unfortunate but true that 'progress' is becoming a bad word in virtually all sectors of our society."[21] Ken Bannon, an official of the United Automobile Workers union, has written that "the traditional concept that hard work is virtue and a duty...is not applicable to younger workers."[22] New UAW contracts to be negotiated in the summer of 1973 are expected to emphasize job quality even more than pay increases.

As portrayed in a host of official studies, press findings and industry reports, the increasingly familiar "blue-collar blues"[23] of bored, alienated assembly-line workers have spread to a white-collar world of dull, unchallenging jobs. There is fear that worker discontent is so pervasive it may undermine the nation's social and economic structure.

If industrialization, technology, automation and the pursuit of economic growth are responsible for many of the social and environmental problems today, people at their leisure may be responsible for just as many problems in the future. Conservationists and environmentalists are sounding the alarm that the superabundance of recreational activity is clogging the highways, polluting the air, littering the wilderness and helping to destroy serenity, if not ecology.

Concern Over Impact of Leisure on Environment

The affluence and mobility of American families, along with the increased amount of leisure time available to them, create serious problems of overcrowding in the national parks every summer. Americans paid an estimated 212 million visits to the

---

[21] Gordon F. Bloom, "Productivity, Weak Link in Our Economy," *Harvard Business Review*, January-February 1971, p. 5.

[22] Letter to Ford Motor Company executive Malcolm L. Denise, made public Feb. 4, 1972.

[23] See "Blue-Collar America," *E.R.R.*, 1970 Vol. II, pp. 629-646.

parks in 1972, mostly by automobile. Traffic becomes snarled for miles in heavily used parks. The Great Smoky Mountains National Park in North Carolina and Tennessee, the most heavily patronized of all, has the dubious distinction of being the first national park in the world to install a traffic light.

Visitors leave billions of pieces of litter scattered around campsites, along roads and even in the remote back country. John McPhee wrote that "People throw trash over the rim of the Grand Canyon.... In Yellowstone, visitors throw junk into the thermal pools.... The Park Service has used a scuba team to collect all the junk that tourists throw into the Merced River, in Yosemite Valley. Cans and bottles retrieved from Lake Powell, in Utah, fill five barges a week."[24]

The development of lightweight camping equipment has produced a boom in backpacking into the wilderness. So many campers strike off into California's Sierra Nevadas that some of the streams and lakes have become polluted as a result of the runoff from pit privies. Secretary of the Interior Rogers C. B. Morton told the House Interior Subcommittee on National Parks and Recreation, Feb. 3, 1972, that pollution abatement programs originally expected to cost the Park Service $36 million would actually cost $69 million. Morton said funds intended for park development had been diverted to pollution control.[25]

The three-day weekend is a matter of deep concern to naturalists. Robin W. Doughty wrote: "The inevitable result of so much time off and increased mobility will be a severe case of people pollution. Omnipresent man, not population growth, becomes the quintessential problem. Mobility, money, technology and leisure are dancing together in a seemingly infinite spiral: technology provides leisure, leisure generates money...money buys mobility...."

> The effects of a burgeoning multitude in search of undefined pleasures are readily apparent [Doughty continued]. Mounds of trash are being spread across the landscape; lines of cars are clogging roads every fair weekend.... Uncontrolled construction of everything from golf course condominiums to AIA-designed beach houses and elaborate resort villages is creating a staggering number of personal mini-gardens of leisurely pleasure—often at the terrible expense of what little unspoiled land remains.[26]

---

[24] John McPhee, "Profiles," *The New Yorker*, Sept. 11, 1971, p. 84.

[25] See "National Parks Centennial," *E.R.R.*, 1972 Vol. I, pp. 128-130.

[26] Robin W. Doughty, "The Three-Day American Pleasure Trip," *Natural History*, June-July 1972, p. 22.

Doughty and others suggest similar "high-intensity" recreation centers at the rim of metropolitan areas for campers, water enthusiasts and for those who prefer to "recreate" with off-road vehicles like dune buggies and snowmobiles. "Some leisure-prone Americans" Doughty wrote, "have long treated the outdoors as alleyways and playgrounds. For them, nature is incidental to the picnic table, the motorized trail bike, the radio and beach buggy...if the growing numbers of people with free time are not given an opportunity to find their own pleasure domes, then wilderness and wildlife, as well as those who love both, will be the losers."

The combination of affluence and leisure has revised the traditional family dream of a second car to also include a second home—a weekend, vacation and future retirement retreat in the mountains, at the lake or seashore. The American Land Development Association, a trade organization, has counted 9,000 vacationland development firms in the United States. They sold 650,000 vacation lots in 1971, the latest year for which figures are available. What troubles the environmentalist is that the natural scenery tends to disappear under the weight of second-home development. The state of Vermont and several communities throughout the nation have taken steps to limit or control the "invasion" of second homes.[27]

Arguments Over Value of Additional Free Time

Concern about the prospects of increased leisure began in the 1950s. Robert Bendiner reported in 1957: "From the spate of literature on the coming Era of Leisure, it is hard to tell whether we are headed for an Elysium of culture that will put the ancient Greeks in the shade or for a hell of mass boredom modified by home carpentry, hi-fi, plus motels and Ping-Pong." William Russell, president emeritus of Teachers College, Columbia University, said at that time that "Too much leisure with too much money has been the dread of societies across the ages. That is when nations cave in from within. That is when they fall."[28]

The Chamber of Commerce of the United States argued in 1962 that if increments of leisure time were misused "in the form of unguided idleness, it will both lower the tone of the community and strain police and other regulatory facilities."

---

[27] For background on land-use problems, see "Protection of the Countryside," *E.R.R.*, 1971 Vol. II, pp. 543-564, and "Restrictions on Urban Growth," *E.R.R.*, 1973 Vol. I, pp. 87-104.

[28] Quoted by Robert Bendiner, "Could You Stand a Four-Day Week?" *The Reporter*, Aug. 8, 1957, p. 10.

ESTIMATED DIVISION OF LEISURE TIME

	Year 1900	Year 2000
Daily	41%	34%
Weekend	28	44
Vacation	10	16
Retired	3	5
Other	18	1

SOURCE: Mary A. Holman, "A National Time-Budget for the year 2000," *Sociology and Social Research (1961)*

On a national level, a shorter workweek would "inevitably raise total labor costs," and this, in turn, would damage the nation's ability to achieve a higher rate of economic growth. Furthermore, the Chamber argued, the availability of more free time could harm rather than help family relationships since "wives and children may resent having the husband and father 'under foot' for a greater part of the day."[29]

Millard C. Faught, writing in 1970, saw the matter differently. He thought that greater leisure would lead to a resurgence in arts and crafts. Faught, chief economist of the Timewealth Corporation in Houston, suggests that the workweek will eventually be reduced to three days, permitting workers to live far away from their jobs. The worker might commute to work only once a week, rent an apartment or "barracks facility" where he would sleep two nights a week. The rest of his time would be spent continuously with his family. "I envisage," Faught added, "a veritable resurgence of all the traditional self-help and group-help patterns of frontier life out there on those new frontiers in Hinterlurbia, when these four-day-weekend pioneers get there."[30]

Paul A. Samuelson foresees a wider choice of options for the ordinary man, to work long or short hours as he pleases. This is "an area where modern man has had the fewest personal options," Samuelson wrote. "If other people work nine to five, then you must conform at the peril of being denied your daily bread."[31] While many persons on a short workweek would unquestionably spend the time off in leisure, others would choose to hold two jobs—as do between three and four million workers today.

---

[29] "A Shorter Workweek," a monograph published by the Chamber of Commerce of the United States in 1962, pp. 12-13.

[30] Millard C. Faught, "The 3-Day Revolution to Come: 3-Day Workweek, 4-Day Weekend," *4 Days, 40 Hours*, p. 139.

[31] Paul A. Samuelson, introduction to *4-Days, 40 Hours.*

Whether for better or worse, more leisure time is in the offing for all who want it. Economist Walter Buckingham writes that before today's workers retire, the workweek may be halved. He notes that this is a cautious estimate compared with many, including that of Joseph Prendergast, director of the National Recreation Association, who forecast a seven-hour workweek within a century.[32]

Problems of Adjusting to Leisure in Retirement

The problems of a future leisure society may be similar to those found in present-day retirement communities. Many of the residents in these communities complain of boredom, lack of purpose and a feeling of uselessness. Ernest Hemingway argued that retirement was "the most loathsome word" in the language. To suddenly lose the work that once consumed the largest part of his life was spiritual annihilation. Melvin Maddocks wrote the retired American worker has a "roleless role." From nursery school on, he is taught the value of a 'productive' life, the ideal of the 'work ethic.' Then at 60 or 65 he is cut off from participation—from the activity he has depended upon for self esteem."[33]

The retirement village is yet another part of the multi-billion dollar "Good Life Industry." There are hundreds of such centers for elderly people across the country. So far, according to *The Wall Street Journal*, "only a few hundred thousand" of America's 20 million retired persons live in them. Robert E. Rosenwald, executive vice president of Rossmoor Corp.—which has developed five leisure villages for the retired—expects that the over-50 population will rise to about 50 million in the next eight years. "Even if only 1 per cent of that number wanted to live in retirement communities," he said, "we couldn't meet the demand."[34]

Retirement communities are seen by some as the prototype of a coming leisure society. While there are any number of activities and amusements available to fill the hours, many retirees are bored and feel acutely the lack of a useful role. Freedom from the necessity of holding down a job will be liberation, according to Melvin Maddocks, "only if alternatives to common everyday work are taken as seriously as work itself." Otherwise, Maddocks and other observers contend, the promised leisure society will offer more predicaments than opportunities.

---

[32] Walter Buckingham, *Automation* (1961), p. 151.
[33] Melvin Maddocks, *The Christian Science Monitor*, Aug. 12, 1972.
[34] Quoted by Hal Lancaster in *The Wall Street Journal*, Nov. 16, 1972.